Good Press

Good Press

An insider's guide to publicizing business
and community news

Richard V Tuttell

Writers Club Press
San Jose New York Lincoln Shanghai

Good Press
An insider's guide to publicizing business and community news

Writers Club Press
an imprint of iUniverse.com, Inc.

For information address:
iUniverse.com, Inc.
620 North 48th Street, Suite 201
Lincoln, NE 68504-3467
www.iuniverse.com

ISBN: 0-595-13024-0

Printed in the United States of America

DEDICATION

To Janelou Buck who showed me the best and worst of
being a community newspaper editor.

EPIGRAPH

A good editor has a sharp nose for what to put into a newspaper and even sharper nose for what to leave out.

Judy Mann
Columnist
1999

CONTENTS

ACKNOWLEDGEMENTS

My thanks to Robert Scott, a publishing consultant and fellow journalist who provided invaluable critiques of the early drafts of this manuscript and book proposal. Thanks to The Freedom Forum's First Amendment Calendar for providing many of the quotes used in the following pages, and Dr. Sharon Pennell and Dr. Janice Pope of Appalachian State University (Boone, N.C.) for sharing both their academic and practical real-world insights. Appreciation is also extended to the many editors with whom I have worked during the last 20 years and, of course, the readers who continue to teach me what role a community newspaper serves, and should serve, in their lives.

Introduction

There are three things
that no one can do to the
entire satisfaction of anyone
else: make love, poke the fire
and run a newspaper.

William Allen White
newspaper editor, 1917

Editors are asked only two questions by readers who complain about the content of their local community newspaper:

- Why did you put that in the paper?

- Why didn't you put that in the paper?

A common variation on the former is: Why did you put that in the paper *that way?*

But essentially, from the thousands of angry phone calls, the heated in-person confrontations both in the office and out in the public, and the nasty letters, it all boils down to those two queries. Of course, they can be phrased in many ways such as:

- What the heck are you people thinking?

- How can you possibly write something like that?
- Where did you get that from?
- Why can't you ever get anything right?
- Why did you do that to Uncle Harry and Aunt Mary's anniversary announcement?

And the ever popular:

- I hope you people down there have a good lawyer.

Good Press addresses all these questions and more. It is intended to help mediate conflicts between the public and community newspapers and other media by explaining how they can work together to their mutual benefit. The primary emphasis is on newspapers because they offer businesses, organizations and individuals the greatest opportunity for free promotion. Information is also included, however, about a variety of broadcast media.

Why focus so much on the print side? There are close to 9,700 newspapers publishing from one to seven times a week in the United States, according to the Newspaper Association of America (NAA). The great majority of those—about 8,200—are weekly or other non-daily papers, and more than 85 percent of the dailies have a circulation of 50,000 or less. They all have an intense interest in—and a vital need for—everyday community news. Even metropolitan dailies with a large number of subscribers realize the value of local items. Dailies today give more front-page coverage to stories originating in their own backyards and less to world news than those of a generation ago, according to a study conducted by University of Maryland Professor Carl Sessions Stepp. In addition, many large newspapers produce zoned editions covering neighborhoods on the fringes of their circulation areas. Newspapers, especially small town publications, depend on public submissions for much of their content and much of that *news*—whether it be business openings, engagement announcements or club meeting notices—generates reader interest that helps sell papers.

Readers, on the other hand, depend on their local newspapers for information not available from any other source. Dick Mitchell, publisher of the News-Topic in Lenoir, N.C., has a favorite saying about local newspapers in small towns: "People already know everything that goes on, they want to read the newspaper to find out who got caught."

It is doubtful that network TV news has the time or inclination to mention on its evening program a weekend yard sale in Cornelia, Ga., that will benefit a local leukemia victim. That news item probably wouldn't rate a mention on the nearest network affiliate and maybe not even on an area radio network. And while the Internet posts more information from around the world than anyone will ever have time to access, it is not going to report all the local community news that you and your neighbors want and need. It probably won't tell you for instance:

• What caused that dark smoke in the sky that sent fire trucks and police cars screaming across town yesterday afternoon.

• What well-known local resident was arrested for shoplifting or other infractions.

• What area business was honored with an industry-wide customer service award.

• Who was named homecoming queen at the local high school.

• Why your county or city tax bill is going up this year.

• Where you can go to protest a zoning change that could put a topless bar in your neighborhood.

- When and where public health officials are going to begin offering flu shots.

- How your kid's baseball team did in its last game.

It is apparent that many readers realize this. A recent nationwide poll that tracked a decline in network TV news viewership also reported some interesting things about newspaper readers' views. The Associated Press reported that according to the survey by the Pew Research Center For The People & The Press, "...credibility was highest for the respondent's home-town paper...."

A national reader survey showed that despite a high level of skepticism of newspaper reporters, Americans said they have a growing need for news. Seventy percent say they find news helpful when making practical decisions, and 88 percent say their need for news stayed constant or grew in the past year.

And how do newspapers themselves view the importance of covering and reporting local news? Of 318 national publishers and editors surveyed by *Presstime* magazine, all rated local news as having "high or very high" appeal to their readers. *Presstime* is the magazine of the NAA.

From my experience, however, I know that people have a love-hate relationship with their newspapers and mass media in general. At the same time many readers would agree that their local paper plays a vital role in keeping everyone informed and serving as a common platform for voicing community concerns and sharing experiences.

While newspapers have been around a lot longer than electronic information providers, a great many people still lack an understanding of how a newspaper functions and how they can best use it to their advantage. Newspapers also share the blame for not doing enough to help their communities understand how they operate.

The primary objective of every newspaper is to communicate to its readers. No matter how well written, how creative the design, how colorful the pages and how respected the name, if a message is not conveyed the newspaper has failed. Much responsibility for that communication's success lies in the sources of the information relied upon by the paper. An applicable computer phrase is: "Garbage in, garbage out." The best way to ensure your newspaper reports the information you want published correctly is to provide it in a clear written form. Now that's no guarantee that everything will come out perfectly in print. No matter how sophisticated the production of a newspaper becomes, there is still going to be a human element involved. Mistakes happen, but helping to streamline the process by which news is provided for publication can minimize them.

Everyone has a need to use a local means of mass media at some point in their lives between the time their birth announcements are printed and their obituaries are published. For example:

• Businesses need to publicize openings, new services, awards and employee promotions.

• Civic clubs need to announce their meeting dates and activities.

• Homeowners and condominium associations need to make public announcements of general interest.

• Churches often want to let the community at large know about a special service or program of interest to more than their own congregation members.

• City, county, state and federal officials need to issue notices about government programs available to citizens or other news of public interest.

• A local or national organization may want to give a resident an honor or recognition in a public forum.

"Good Press" suggests the best ways to facilitate that communication. It is based on my 20 years of editing community newspapers, contacts with editors from a variety of other newspapers large and small, surveys, and additional research. While the term "community newspaper" is used by some in the industry to refer only to non-dailies, I use it to encompass all papers that set a high priority on covering and reporting their city's, county's or region's local news. Unless otherwise noted, this information submitted to these local newspapers is published free of charge. Sample forms (see Appendix C) provide an idea of the format and type of information many papers require for printing engagement and wedding announcements, obituary notices and business news.

This form of communication that has been described as being black and white and read all over may be facing much more competition from the electronic sources in the 21st century, but there is a widespread belief that it will stick around for a while because of the impact it has on our lives. It's therefore not a bad idea for everyone to learn a little about what makes this beast tick.

1. NEWS RELEASE BASICS

A News-Paper...ought to be the Register of the times, and faithful recorder of every species of intelligence; it ought not to be engrossed by any particular object; but, like a well-covered table, it should contain something suited to every palate...and by steering clear of extremes, hit the happy medium.

Daily Universal Register
1785

The woman with the soft voice on the other end of the phone line appeared to have been taken aback by the man's suggestion.

"Oh, I don't think I could do that," she said.

"Sure you can," he responded.

"But...I've never done this before. I wouldn't know where to start. Are you sure I can't just do it with you over the phone? You know all the right things to say and just how to put it."

Finally, he managed to convince the caller that no matter how uncomfortable she was with the idea, as a newspaper editor, he was confident she could do it all by herself.

Such is the intimidation often encountered when it comes to submitting a news release (also known as a press release). It is important that people get over that initial reluctance, because there is no way that editors or reporters by themselves can produce all the hundreds of items that go into a weekly or daily newspaper. As a policy, many newspapers require releases in writing to help ensure accuracy and resolve disputes later about what information was submitted and what eventually made it into print. While some papers can accept short dictated announcements, many reporters and editors do not have the time to take community news items over the phone, and they don't want to increase the chances of getting anything wrong.

You don't have to be a professional writer to produce an effective news release. And you don't have to work for a fancy public relations firm— although the money you might make at one would be nice. (Copywriters can reportedly get $20 to $30 per hour for producing press releases.) Some newspapers don't even require information to be sent in complete sentences. All, however, prefer that a message be clearly stated and the information be well organized so that it can be easily read and understood.

All you need to do is write out the answers to six questions about the event or item you want publicized. They are *who, what, when, where, why* and *how* (not necessarily in that order). You may not even have to answer all six. You might find that you can get your message across without the "how" and "why," for instance.

Let's look at each question:

• **Who.** This usually is the name of the person or organization publicizing the item or sponsoring the event. For example:

> ***The Service Club*** will hold a
> potluck dinner Tuesday, Aug. 7, at 6
> p.m. at the clubhouse located at 22
> Twain Ave. in Townville.

- **What.** This is the reason for the release. It is the thing being publicized.

> The Service Club will hold a **potluck dinner** Tuesday, Aug. 7, at 6 p.m. at the clubhouse located at 22 Twain Ave. in Townville.

- **Where.** This is the location of the event or activity being publicized or the address or phone number of the place to direct donations, information or questions. Always include a street address because not everyone might know, for example, where the B.G. Wingding Civic Center is located.

> The Service Club will hold a potluck dinner Tuesday, Aug. 7, at 6 p.m. at the **clubhouse located at 22 Twain Ave. in Townville.**
>
> For more information or to reserve tickets call the Service Club at **555-1111.**

- **When.** This the date and time of the event and any deadlines that may apply.

> The Service Club will hold a potluck dinner **Tuesday, Aug. 7, at 6 p.m.** at the clubhouse located at 22 Twain Ave. in Townville.
>
> Advance tickets will be $5 and can be purchased up until **noon on the day of the dinner.** Tickets at the door will be $6.

> For more information or to reserve tickets call the Service Club at 555-1111.

• **Why**. This is an explanation of the reasons the event or activity is being held.

> The Service Club will hold a potluck dinner Tuesday, Aug. 7, at 6 p.m. at the clubhouse located at 22 Twain Ave. in Townville. **The dinner is being held to fund scholarships for local students.**
>
> Advance tickets will be $5 and can be purchased up until noon on the day of the dinner. Tickets at the door will be $6.
>
> For more information or to reserve tickets call the Service Club at 555-1111.

• **How**. The answer to this question might be included to give directions to the event or to explain how the activity will be organized or presented.

> The Service Club will hold a potluck dinner Tuesday, Aug. 7, at 6 p.m. at the clubhouse located at 22 Twain Ave. in Townville. The dinner is being held to fund scholarships for local students.
>
> Advance tickets will be $5 and can be purchased up until noon on

the day of the dinner. Tickets at the door will be $6.

To get to the clubhouse take Highway 7 south and turn left on Barbecue Road. The dinner will be served in a buffet style.

For more information or to reserve tickets call the Service Club at 555-1111.

OKay, it's not all that simple. Additional tips about news releases are provided in the following chapters, but for now at least you know the basics.

2. BUILDING A BETTER NEWS RELEASE

*The media represent a
tremendous opportunity for
unpaid publicity.*

Roland Rust
Marketing professor
1994

One of the great things about working in a newspaper office is that you never know what kind of story lead will come across your desk next. It might be a grisly murder, a devastating natural disaster, or a church bake sale. A bake sale is every bit as important to the organizers of that event—maybe more important than the murder and the disaster. It is important to a community newspaper too.

Joe Charles visited the newspaper office one day concerned that a notice that had been dropped off about his group's meeting had not yet appeared in the paper. It was easy enough to track the release. The news editor had handed it to the reporter who had written earlier stories on the group's efforts. The notice had stalled at that reporter's desk and one look at the release showed why.

"Specific objectives of the Group
of Concerned Citizens of Everytown
are to positively influence and to

improve conditions and awareness in the following areas of our communities: Economic and educational development; political awareness on local, state and national levels; physical and mental health; equal justice under the law.

"The main thrust of the organization is to encourage involvement in the political process so that all citizens may have a sense of empowerment and control over their lives."

Then, at the bottom of the page, appeared the paragraph pertaining to that week's meeting. A statement about the group's purpose is useful, but it doesn't provide any immediate sense of urgency to an editor or reporter. Sure, it would have only taken a minute for a staff member to read down to the dated information, but a deadline mentality often puts newsrooms into a mode of making quick priority assessments. It's not always the best way to operate, but there are reasons things are done this way.

With the number of news releases coming in the door, through the mail, over the fax machine and being sent electronically, news staffs—especially those in downsized editorial departments—have to process a lot of information as quickly as possible. An item that doesn't appear pressing at first glance may be set aside in favor of something else that is clearly timelier. This is what happened to the Concerned Citizens' news release. Because it started out with a broad statement rather than the imminent meeting date, it wasn't recognized as needing immediate attention.

Anyone submitting a release should organize the information to make sure the urgency of the piece is spelled out right away. In the case of Mr. Charles's news release, the editor made sure it appeared in the next day's edition prior to that night's meeting. The published notice, however, began with the information on the meeting time and place. Readers, like editors, often won't spend more than a few seconds on an item to determine whether it has any interest to them. Studies have shown that readers spend as little as 30 seconds glancing at an entire newspaper page when deciding whether there's anything on it they want to read.

Leading a news release with the date of an event, however, is not always the best way to go if there is an earlier deadline for getting tickets or registering for the activity being publicized. For example:

> The local chapter of the Friends of the Antelope will be having its annual dinner dance on Friday, May 8, at the Watering Hole Room beginning at 7:30 p.m.
>
> The dinner will feature a hot buffet and the night's entertainment will be provided by Eddie and the Melody Makers performing popular songs of the '70s. The Watering Hole Room is located at the corner of Jeckle and Hyde avenues.
>
> Reservations for the dinner must be made no later than May 1.

An editor working on deadline who is hurriedly scanning the computer directory for some timely briefs for the April 30 edition may bring up the "Friends" item on his computer screen and then return the file to the holding area because, after all, it's still April and this event isn't being held for more than a week. Apparently it can wait, while there may be something coming up sooner that should take priority. What is missed in this case, because it is buried at the end of the piece, is the operative date of **May 1**. Here's how the release could have been more effectively presented:

The deadline for reservations to the Friends of the Antelope annual dinner-dance is Friday, May 1.

The event will be held May 8, at the Watering Hole Room beginning at 7:30 p.m. It will feature a hot buffet, and Eddie and Melody Makers performing popular songs of the '70s will provide the night's entertainment.

The Watering Hole Room is located at the corner of Jeckle and Hyde avenues.

Here are some other tips to help make sure news releases get the attention of the editor:

• **Type or print.** It doesn't matter that everyone else on the planet says they can read your writing, you've never had a problem communicating by the written word before and you've won the World's Most Attractive Handwriting Competition for the last five years. Typing, or at least printing, a release can save a lot of grief for a typesetter or news clerk who is trying to accurately input information into a computer. Optical scanners also have a much easier time recognizing typed words. There will be more about this in Chapter 4.

• **Double-space or triple-space your lines of type.** This gives the editor room to make editing marks on the page to customize the copy to fit the newspaper's style or to correct typos. Also leave a one to a one and a half inch margin on all sides of the copy and at least two inches at the top of the page for editor's notes and directions to the typesetter.

- **Clearly identify**. Always put the name or the organization, school or person involved in the body of the copy. This may seem obvious, but often news releases are submitted with this information printed only on the envelope or the letterhead, neither of which may be seen by the editor. All he may see is the computer file that is set by the news clerk or typesetter from the original material.

- **Don't assume anything**. Write the dates of events, deadlines or meetings, not just "tonight" or "Monday," because by the time the release gets typeset and routed to the proper computer file, a day or two may have passed. Having the dates on the items also makes it easier for the newspaper to prioritize news and make sure releases that are out of date are not published.

When using a non-standard spelling of a name or other word make note of it near the top of the release. Editors are trained to detect anything out of the ordinary and many might change the word or name to a more traditional spelling. Some newspapers advise publicity chairpersons to put a pencil check mark above names with untraditional spellings to let the editor know that the name is correct. Others suggest using the notation "OK" or "CO" to indicate the unusual spelling is correct. Don't assume that editors or readers know what initials or abbreviations mean. Reporters sometimes even have trouble with this. They may have written so many articles on the DNR that by now they think everyone knows it stands for the Department of Natural Resources. Not every reader knows that. Always write out the full name in the first reference.

Include all the background needed for a news release to make sense. Don't assume everyone already knows what you mean or that the editor will fill in any information gaps. Old-timers may be aware of how to find an event by being told that it is across the street from where the old Esso service station used to be. Newcomers and others with shorter memories need an exact address.

• **Timing**. We'll get more into details on deadlines in a later chapter, but basically make sure you allow plenty of notice of an upcoming event. Keep in mind that publication deadlines are often staggered for different sections of the newspaper, so what might be early for the front section may be too late for the lifestyle pages.

• **Stick to one message**. Each news release should tell only one story. Try to include too much and the main point of the release may be missed or cause confusion in the editor's—and eventually in the reader's—mind.

• **Use simple words**. Stay away from jargon or technical language that many readers (and many editors for that matter) aren't likely to understand. Government bureaucrats can be the worst offenders. For example, city officials may plan "to implement a proposal to provide for the installation of electronically-controlled signalization to intersecting primary roadways." In other words, they want to put a stop light at the street corner.

• **Be literal.** Some people still insist on believing everything they read, so stick to the exact meanings of the words you use. A news release on an antique car show that states the event "will feature a ton of automobiles" tells the readers there won't be more than one car at the show if that statement is taken literally. That's because a single vehicle can easily weigh a ton.

• **Use standard English.** Contractions such as can't, wouldn't and she's are such a regular part of our speech that we often don't even realize we're using them. And while their meanings are easily understood, they are too informal for a news release. The only place they might be appropriate is in a quote.

• **Keep sentences short.** Taking small bites makes it easier to digest food, and it is the same when digesting reading material. Editors will usually break up run-on sentences anyway, and they may not divide them the way you would prefer. So stick to one simple thought in each sentence and provide one less excuse for an editor to alter what you have written.

• **Avoid using an italic or other fancy typeface.** When using a computer or other word processor, choose a typeface that is as close to a standard typewriter face as possible to ensure readability by a newspaper editor, typesetter or scanning device. When printing your document it is best to use a letter-quality printer.

• **Don't send a flier**. A flier or poster containing information on an event is not a news release; it is just a flier or poster. By submitting this type of promotional material to the newspaper you hand over all control of how the information will be presented in the paper. And it may not get in at all because it takes additional time and effort to put it into a narrative form. A woman who turned in a flier on an upcoming Christian rally was disappointed that the youth aspect of the rally was not emphasized in the first paragraph of the published news item. The next time she made sure to submit a news release that put her youth priority at the top. This also goes for fact sheets and information submitted in a tabular format that require some editing directions before it can even be typeset. Instead, take a few minutes and write out what you want to say the way you want it to be said.

• **Suggested headlines.** It is a good idea to suggest a headline for a news item, but remember that space and style requirements can require changes. Also, don't leave out essential information in the body of the copy just because it appears in the title, because if the headline is not used, that information may be omitted upon publication. This happened once with a release on a driving class that told the location of the training session in the suggested headline but didn't mention it anywhere else in the copy.

• **Use standard-size sheets of paper.** While recycling is a noble endeavor, sending in a news release on the flap from a frozen dinner entree is going a bit too far. Submitting a release on a Post-It note, scrap of paper or back of an old envelope is a good way to decrease the chances of ever seeing that information in print. Use a standard-size sheet of paper (8 ½ by 11 inches) because most offices are geared toward handling such documents. Odd-shaped sheets of paper, especially small scraps, can too easily slide into crevices between office furniture never to be seen again, except maybe when the newsroom gets around to doing a thorough cleaning. In other words—never.

• **Use a legal-sized envelope.** Using a longer envelope allows the standard letter-sized sheet to only be folded twice, making the release easier to unfold and neater for the editor to read.

• **Be brief.** Get to the primary reason of the release as soon as possible. For example, don't start off with a long list of sponsors before getting to the event being sponsored. Remember that a news release should be concise, providing only essential information. Answer the basic questions (who, what, where, when, why and how) in the first two paragraphs. Releases that are too long may require some editing to fit the available space. It is always better if the person submitting the release do the editing in advance because he is more aware of the importance of each bit of information. Also, shorter news releases often have a good chance of getting into the paper faster because there are more small holes to fill than larger ones. But don't go overboard with brevity. A line that gives readers a telephone number for more information should not be a substitute for the basic who, what, where, when and why.

• **Include a name and phone number**. Editors need to know how to reach a contact person in case there's a question about the news item. Not including a contact name is one of the most common news release mistakes cited by newspaper editors. Make sure, however, that it is clear whether a phone number included on the release is for publication or is only for use by the newspaper. Often it is a good idea to provide a number for publication that a reader can call for more information, because, depending on the amount of news space available, some details may have to be cut by the editor.

• **Note the time requested for release.** Unless it is clearly marked for later publication, an editor will assume a news release is ready for print when it is received, and will determine the timing of the publication depending on a variety of factors. Make arrangements with an editor before sending a release that requires a specific publication date. As a general rule, however, if the information is not ready for release, don't release it.

• **Don't be too descriptive.** Save descriptive adjectives for feature stories and personal opinions for the editorial page. News releases should contain the basic details of the bike race event, not statements about the beautiful scenery the bike riders will enjoy along the route. Use nouns and verbs to tell the story.

• **Use quotes when appropriate.** If a description or opinion must be included, put it in quotes and attribute it to someone. Avoid attributing a quote to more than one person. Releases that have whole paragraphs of quotes attributed to two or more people will cast doubt in the minds of editors and readers about the credibility of the piece because it is highly unlikely that people will say a series of words in unison. Also with quotes, keep the attribution simple. Most newspaper writers will just use, "said Martha Washington," instead of "cried Martha Washington." Be especially wary of loaded words that can taint the reader's perception of the quote. Attributions such as "she claimed," can color the meaning of the speaker's words in the reader's mind.

• **Don't get personal.** Use the third person voice in writing a release because that is how it will appear in print. The use of phrases such as "We are having our picnic lunch at our clubhouse," can give the impression to readers that the newspaper is hosting the lunch at its offices when in fact the Women of the Arts group is hosting it. A better way of writing it is, "Members of the Women of the Arts will be having their picnic lunch at their clubhouse."

• **Be accurate.** It is the responsibility of the news release writer to present the facts. Readers, however, hold newspapers responsible for all errors of fact so even press release mistakes can hurt a paper's reputation. In such cases the credibility of the person submitting the releases will also be tarnished as will his ability to get future releases into print.

• **Advise editors of multiple pages.** While most notices should not require more than one page, if there are other pages to the release write or type "(More)" at the bottom of the page. This may seem obvious, but the beleaguered editor who is handling a large stack of releases may not have time to wonder for long why a one-page announcement ends with an incomplete sentence. Any help is appreciated. To designate the end of the copy a "-30-" or "###" is easily understood by editors.

• **Advise editors of photos.** If a photograph has been supplied with the news release, make a note of it on the release. It can be a simple statement such as "With art" or a more detailed description such as "Photo included of woman with meatloaf in soup kitchen." Send the photo and the release together. Don't expect the paper to hold a release while waiting for the accompanying art. More information on photos and captions is provided in Chapter 8.

• **Note any costs.** If there is a charge associated with the event being publicized make sure the cost is mentioned. Otherwise, the reader may assume it is free. Keep in mind that the fact that an event that is open to the public or is hosted by a non-profit organization can figure into the decision to print or broadcast a public service announcement. A former editor used to throw a fit when someone would write, "A $5 donation will be collected at the door." She would argue that a donation is a gift that is voluntarily given and if it costs $5 to get in the door that is an admission charge, not a donation.

• **Emphasize the local aspect.** Editors must be convinced a release deserves space in the newspaper because of its interest to local readers. A paper received a release once about someone in a town 200 miles away who was awarded a scholarship. The release neglected to mention that this person had grown up and attended school in the paper's hometown. By the time his local parents had called to ask about publication of the item it had already been discarded because it had no apparent local connection.

• **Till further notice.** This is an expression often used in the classified advertising department to mean that the ad should continue to run until notice is given to stop. People who submit news releases shouldn't expect similar treatment. There is a finite amount of space or "news hole" in a newspaper and often several other releases are competing for that space, so it may be difficult if not impossible to keep repeating the same news. Many papers may have a community calendar section that accommodates such items and may allow them to be repeated.

• **Proof of publication.** A reader once called about the publication status of a news release she had dropped off a few days before. It was a notice about the application process for a government program that she said had to run as soon as possible. The editor told her he would do his best to get it in as space permitted, and she demanded that she be notified when it finally did run. Another person called about a similar release that he said had to run exactly as submitted in order to satisfy state notification requirements. Few, if any, newspaper editors will run an item without making sure it conforms to the needs and style of the paper (see Chapter 5). And fewer still have the time to notify sources about the scheduled publication times of news items. If an article must be printed on a certain day or worded in a particular way to satisfy some procedural or legal publication requirement, or if official notice of publication must be provided, it should be submitted as a paid advertisement, not as a news release. If that is the intent, make sure it is clearly marked "for advertising" on the envelope as this type of information often requires prompt attention.

• **Phoning it in.** In a word, don't. As noted in the preceding chapter, many newspapers will not take news releases over the phone. That's because the potential for misunderstandings and mistakes is too great, especially in communicating essential information such as who and when. The potential for misspelling of names alone is enough to justify such a policy. At a newspaper in Wilkes-Barre, Pa., an elderly fill-in obituary taker who had a hearing problem exemplified what can happen. In one obit, the deceased was reported to have worked for the Dorr-Oliver Company. In the newspaper, however, he was listed as having been employed by the Do it All Over Again Company. There is also a lack of accountability if the person calling in the release later complains of an error. It may be difficult to track the cause of the problem because of a lack of a paper trail or electronic record. An example of where a hard copy came in handy was when a newspaper had a complaint about the wrong name having been used in a wedding announcement. The fact that the name belonged to the mayor's son only added to the embarrassment. After hearing from the irate mayor it was discovered that the written form submitted for the announcement included the erroneous name that had been published. The paper still printed a correction, but at least the news staff—and the mayor—knew the cause of that mistake. A final reason for requiring written releases is that many papers with limited staffs don't have the resources to assign someone to sit at a desk and take news release information over the phone.

• **Save a copy**. Keep a copy of what is sent to the newspaper. This is a good idea for three reasons. First, it provides proof of exactly what was submitted in case there should be a dispute later over whether important information was erroneously omitted or altered in the printed version. Second, if the release is lost on the way to the paper, or after arriving there, it can be resubmitted. And third, the writer can compare the original to what was printed in the paper to learn how to better adapt future releases to the style and requirements of the newspaper.

• **Sending press kits**. Most individuals don't have to go to the trouble or expense of putting together a press kit. This type of package, however, can be helpful in publicizing a series of events or announcements. For instance, if a new industry is locating or expanding in the county, a press kit can provide detailed background on the company and its plans. When a performer is coming to town, a kit containing feature story ideas, contact names, photos and biographies can come in handy. Sports teams and events may also benefit from the use of press kits with rosters and player records. This also can be a good way to provide photos that would not be easily obtainable by the newspaper staff. But no matter how attractive the package, remember it is content that counts. Many slick, and obviously expensively produced, press kit folders go from the mail to the trash can in short order because they don't contain anything of local interest to the newspaper's readers.

3. DEADLINES

There's nothing like a newspaper newsroom to give you a well-rounded education.

Ora Eddleman
Newspaper editor
1895

Every child should be taught three things as soon as possible after birth:

- Don't touch a hot stove.

- Look both ways before crossing the street.

- Don't bother an editor on deadline.

Experienced members of my former newsroom knew enough to brace themselves upon hearing the telephone ring on Tuesday morning. We were rarely spared the inevitable eruption from the office of our executive editor Janelou Buck.

"IT'S TUESDAY!"

That exasperated exclamation conveyed several messages. To the switchboard operator it translated into, "This had better be important because everyone on the planet should realize that I'm on deadline and am extremely busy trying to get a paper out." To the rest of the newsroom (and anyone else in earshot, which was usually about everyone else in the building considering Janelou's stage-trained ability to project) it meant, "Can you believe that I'm being interrupted like this when we are actively engaged in the most important responsibility that has ever been delegated to mankind?"

Such delusions, while exaggerated, are actually not so uncommon under deadline pressure. At such times, every bit of a newspaper editor's attention—especially at a small newspaper—is focused on getting his or her collection of words and photos ready for printing and distribution. Just about anything that does not directly affect this process is considered an unwelcome distraction.

It is not a good time, for example, to call to chat about a "blurb" on next Saturday's chicken barbecue or to discuss editorial philosophies. And depending on how close to deadline the staff is, even items that may be newsworthy and in need of getting into the publication in progress may have to be disregarded. Mike Leach, an editor of the Sebring (Fla.) *News-Sun*, had his own test for the type of news story that would justify redoing a page that had been completed just before the deadline. A breaking story would have to be the equivalent of the President of the United States being shot…by the Pope.

Considering that many newspapers contain enough information to fill a book, adherence to deadline is the only way that "the daily miracle" can be successfully performed. Understanding newspaper deadlines, and the emotions they evoke, provides insight about the best time to interact with an editor or news staff. It may explain why editors can at times appear impatient, distracted or even frantic during a phone conversation and why they might try to end the call prematurely. I've often thought of putting a sign on my office door warning: "Editors on deadline may appear grumpier than they actually are." Not that there's ever a good excuse for rudeness, but every minute diverted from the work at hand has the potential of adding a minute to the production schedule and eventually making the paper late.

It's a domino effect, with one piece impacting all the others down the line.

If the news department can't get the page designs, copy, photos, headlines and photo captions to the compositors on time the pages may arrive late to the camera room. The camera room may then be delayed in getting the page negatives to the plate room. This puts the press department behind, creating a high probability that the mailroom or packaging center cannot get the papers inserted and ready for the carriers. Eventually, the subscribers and newsstand customers feel the impact by not getting serviced in a timely manner. When those complaints get back to the publisher he starts looking for what went wrong earlier down the line. Delays affect the publisher's, and the newspaper's, bottom line because many of those people who are waiting around are being paid for their wasted time.

Basically, a deadline is the last possible moment for completing a particular task. Depending on that task, a newspaper deadline period can extend for various amounts of time—an hour, four hours, or even an entire 12-hour workday. One of the most intense deadlines faced by a newspaper editor involves completing the last page or section of that day's or week's edition.

Deadline pressure intensity varies depending on several factors—frequency of publication, staff size and publication time. In Janelou's case, we may have had the worst of all possible situations—a weekly publication, a small staff and a morning deadline.

While putting out a paper only once a week may seem like a relaxed endeavor compared to meeting a daily deadline, that's often not the case. It can be a more hectic experience because the production pressure is concentrated into a shorter period of time. No matter how much advance time is available to plan for the next issue, there are certain things that can only be done on deadline just before publication.

Smaller staffs mean that news staffers at weeklies are often pressed into duties done by other separate departments on bigger papers. A weekly newspaper editor may not only read a reporter's copy, write a headline and decide where the story will go on the page, but also go back to the composing area and help prepare the pages for printing. (Many editors at all-sized papers are getting more involved with page composition because of computer programs that allow them to design the pages on the computer screen.) Some hands-on editors may even spend part of their deadline day in the darkroom processing the photographic negatives they took for that day's edition, or sitting at a computer downloading images from a digital camera, disc or the Internet.

As you can see, an editor of a smaller paper will probably be more involved with the weekly or daily deadline work. On a larger staff, many of these responsibilities are delegated, freeing up the top editors to interact with the public and other departments in a more civil manner during deadline.

A daytime deadline at an afternoon or evening paper can also add pressure. There are so many more potential distractions during the time when the newspaper office is open for business that it can be more difficult to concentrate on the matter at hand. A deadline that occurs at night—after the doors are locked, incoming calls are less frequent, switchboard duties are turned over to an electronic attendant, other departments are devoid of employees and the office is relatively quiet—can make for a more relaxed editor on deadline.

As to when the news staff is actually "on deadline," it varies from paper to paper. A general room of thumb is that morning papers have an evening deadline often extending to midnight or beyond, and afternoon papers have a morning news cycle that ends at 10 or 11 a.m. Large papers often also have an earlier deadline for the edition that goes to surrounding communities and a later deadline for the edition that goes to the metro delivery area.

The closer you get to those "zero hours," the more intense activity becomes and the more focused editors have to be on the job at hand. The best thing to do is to call the paper to find out when the deadlines are and then make a point to work around them when calling on items that are not urgent. That way you will have a better chance of having the editor pay full attention to your information.

I know taking deadlines into consideration before calling would have made the late Janelou Buck very happy, and I suspect it would make a lot of editors' lives a little easier.

Timely submissions

Every editor can relate horror stories about the fax that comes over minutes before the paper goes to press with information about an event or activity happening that day, or the news release received in the mail that was intended to provide "advance" notification of something that already took place the day before. It is frustrating for everyone; because once the window of opportunity for a news item is missed it is gone for good, at least in print form. And having an updated story on a newspaper Web site just isn't the same when the information is not readily accessible to a large portion of the readership without online access.

To avoid these situations, find out about your newspaper's copy submission deadlines, and don't assume that the deadline is the same for all types of news items. Because different sections of a newspaper may be made up in advance there could be different deadlines for church news than club, school, business or entertainment releases. Deadlines for these sections can range from a few days to an entire week before the actual publication date.

With submissions, the general rule is the earlier the better, but being too early can sometimes work against you as well. The deadline mentality that puts a priority on time-sensitive releases can strike again if an item is turned in a month early and is pushed aside for more urgent news, only to be discovered two months later buried under a mound of file clippings, trade magazines and a half-eaten ham and cheese sandwich.

Like any manufacturing process, newspapers have a publication rhythm. Once you find that sweet spot for your submissions you should-n't have much trouble figuring out when to submit an item to ensure prompt and reliable publication.

4. THE PATH OF LEAST RESISTANCE

Journalists usually have a
different perspective on the
world...Most   journalists
never had a real job.

James Gentry
Journalism dean
1994

Why in the world would you want to make a newspaper editor's job any easier?

After all, wasn't it that guy down at the paper who messed up your sister's engagement announcement? And while somebody over there didn't think your kid's day care center's production of "Our Town" was newsworthy enough to send out a photographer and reporter, the publication did deem it important enough to report that little run-in Uncle Jimbob had with the vice squad back in 1992.

So why should you care about helping an editor?

The answer is blatant self-interest.

Sure there may have been some times when you and your community's print media haven't been on the best of terms. But there will undoubtedly be times when it will be to your advantage to use this form of mass communication, as it is often the best means of getting a message out to the greatest number of people in your community. And at such a time you can benefit by making sure it is to the editor's advantage to help you.

The best way to get what you want is to give the editors what they want—a minimum of hassle in handling your news release. Believe it or not, newspaper people are only human, although they may think of themselves as a little bit above that standard while many rate them a lot lower. An average editor is probably already juggling several things at once so the idea is to avoid adding another item that will throw off his rhythm.

Even hard-working editors tend to follow the path of least resistance when given the chance. It is not a matter of being lazy in most cases. It's just being efficient with time and effort. A submission that comes in the door, through the mail slot, over the fax machine or across the Internet in an editor-friendly form is much more likely to get prompt attention and make it into print quicker and more intact than one that has to pass through several preliminary stages.

Here are a few tips to ease the transition from submission to publication:

• **Address mail properly.** Making sure a mailed release gets to the right person as directly as possible increases the chances of it getting proper treatment. You can help your cause a great deal by what you write on the envelope. Much of the mail received by newspapers each day—yes, even by small weeklies—is often sorted several times, first by department and then within the various departments. The process is streamlined when the name of an individual, the specific title of a staff member or the nature of the news item is noted on the envelope. When items are just addressed to the newspaper. (I've even seen some addressed to "Any newspaper" followed by the city and state) the routing is stalled. The initial sorter then has to open the envelope to determine the appropriate department, and then the department head has to check the contents to determine on which desk it belongs. At some papers you may be playing Russian roulette when you just write: "To *The Get'em Gazette*." It's not that newspapers are unorganized but often an element of chaos is involved in a business that thrives on daily or weekly deadlines. That feeling was epitomized in a statement attributed to Roger Mikeal, a copy desk chief at the *Charlotte (N.C.) Observer*, who reportedly quipped, "We don't put the paper out. It escapes."

Things go a little faster if the envelope is addressed to the editor or the news department, but it still slows down the handling more than if it said, "Letter to the editor," or "Community calendar item," or "Business news," or "Church page." The same goes for the words included in the subject line of an e-mail. "Church news" or "Business item" is better than just "Press release." Be as specific as possible in the space allotted.

Mail will eventually get to the right person no matter how it is addressed, but providing a complete address can improve efficiency and make for a happier editor. And just think what a wonderful world this would be if we could make all newspaper editors happier.

• **Update mailing lists**. Every day mail is received at papers addressed to editors who haven't worked at that newspaper for years. If the sender doesn't believe it is important enough to make sure the editor listed in the address is still around, it is only natural that the editor won't think of this communication as important either. That doesn't mean that something coming in like this won't get printed in the paper and another piece addressed to an editor by name will, but it certainly doesn't make a good first impression. Because staffing is often in flux (it is not unheard of for newspapers to go through four or five top editors in five years), it is a good idea to update mailing—or fax or e-mail—lists at least annually. A quick call to the newspaper office or a glance at the newspaper itself, or the paper's Web site, can also provide an update.

• **One release per envelope.** Sending multiple releases in one envelope may save money on postage, but the danger here is that an editor may have no interest in the first page he sees and will toss out everything without realizing there is more than one release there. If more than one release must be sent in a single package, include a summary sheet as the first page that briefly describes each release enclosed. This not only tips off the editor that there is more here than at first meets the eye, it also helps make the sorting process more efficient.

• **Don't "shotgun."** This means don't send copies of the same release to more than one department with the hope of increasing the likelihood of exposure. A recurring example is a National Arbor Day Foundation release that is mailed out to many news editors. At one paper the same release was sent in five separate envelopes each addressed to a different staff member in the newsroom. (You would think this organization would be a little more interested in saving paper and trees.) This practice, also known as double planting, can cause a duplication of effort if several people typeset the same release, and it certainly doesn't endear the sender to the staff.

When in doubt about whether to send the release to the attention of the Lifestyles, Business or Community Calendar departments, just send one copy to the news editor and let him make that call.

With a corrected or updated news release, make sure to indicate clearly the difference between the new submission and the original or an editor may consider it a duplication.

• **DON'T CAPITALIZE EVERY LETTER IN THE RELEASE.** Some people from whom newspapers regularly get releases must have their "Caps Lock" button jammed on their typewriters or computer keyboards. These writers might think it adds emphasis to their report, but all it does is make it harder to read. Remember that the objective is effective communication, and putting everything in all caps, or up style, can defeat the purpose by unnecessarily emphasizing every word.

Proper names and titles that deserve capitalization can get lost in such releases. Remember, sometimes a whisper is more persuasive than a shout. (This also applies to using multiple exclamation points after a sentence!!! Exclamation points should be sparingly used. When absolutely necessary, one conveys the necessary emphasis. Any more than one is overkill. YOU GET MY POINT!?!)

• **Forget the brightly colored paper.** Stick to traditional white paper for press releases and save the fancy stuff for fliers. Sometimes these pastel colors are so bright you can almost read them in the dark. They may be used with hopes of attracting more attention than the basic white stock, but for editors whose eyes are already strained from staring at a computer screen all day, they may only produce headache, dizziness and nausea. And while a grouchy editor's comfort or well-being may not be of much concern to most people, remember that you may be inflicting this suffering on the poor typesetter or news clerk who is delegated the duty of inputting this information into the computer system.

• **Use the friendliest format.** People often ask whether it is all right to submit handwritten items for publication, and most claim their handwriting is readable. It may very well be—to a select number of government decoders.

As noted before, typewritten copy is preferred. Most newspapers, however, accept handwritten material. Newspapers pride themselves on being accessible to the entire community and because not everyone has access to a typewriter, let alone a computer and printer or Internet connection, it is inevitable that some submissions will be produced with pen and paper. The best thing for the writer to do is to print so that the words are communicated as accurately as possible.

The office legend of William Tom Mingo always comes to mind when discussing hand-written submissions. Actually there is no such person as

William Tom Mingo as far as I know, but you wouldn't know that by reading one edition of our newspaper. A news item on the men's chorus performing at a local high school noted that Mr. Mingo was the person to contact for more information about the chorus. Although the bulk of the press release had been typed, the name of the contact person had been signed at the bottom of the paper. Our misreading of the contact person's name was subsequently called to our attention by the publicity chairman for the chorus, William *Tamminga*.

Because of the many variations in spellings, names can be especially tough to decipher from handwriting. And it is important to get the names right, whether it is to give credit where credit is due or to lay blame where it belongs. As the old saw goes, "I don't care what you say about me in the paper, just make sure you spell my name right."

Typing, of course, is better because it doesn't put the paper's typesetter in the precarious position of trying to interpret what the writer really wants to say. Also, many papers now have scanners with optical character recognition (OCR) programs that can read typed pages and transfer the words into the digital language used by computers. These scanners, however, must first recognize the writing. Often these high-tech machines will do the same thing we humans would do if we had trouble reading something—take a guess. For example, scanners have been known to mangle words such as "Baptist" (13aptist), "married" (n?a'Tied), "Dec. 19" ([ec. 19), and "of" (ol').

Eliminating the typesetting or scanning altogether is one of the best ways to send information to newspapers. If you have a computer and it has a modem, find out whether your newspaper has a similar setup and if it can receive your copy in digital form over the telephone line or a cable connection. Many newspapers are accepting copy by e-mail. Such an arrangement may not be practical for people who rarely submit anything to the paper, but it certainly could be worth the trouble for publicity people whose duties include frequent interaction with the local press.

Even if a computer setup doesn't include a telephone modem, information can still be transferred in digital form. Newspapers will often accept a submission on a floppy disk in a text or digital image format that is compatible with their software. (The beauty of using the Internet to transfer files is that everyone is on a common platform, which eliminates the problem of incompatible software.) Always provide a hard copy printout as well in case the digital version gets garbled or can't be accessed. In most cases, by transferring information digitally you're not just saving typesetting time for the paper. It also increases the chance that what you wrote will appear correctly in the publication. An item that is already in the editor's computer is much closer to newsprint than one that's sitting in a stack of papers waiting to be typed or scanned into the system.

• **Know your media.** It doesn't do you or your news release much good to ask for Sunday publication if the newspaper you send it to publishes only Monday through Saturday. Find out the particular publication requirements and limitations of the newspaper with which you are dealing.

• **Know your target audience.** A national education association once sent a package of back-to-school features the week before Labor Day. The problem was this particular county school system had already sent students back to class two weeks before that. The association should have known that school schedules vary around the country. Do your homework to make sure your material reaches the newspaper in a timely manner.

• **Make follow-up calls sparingly.** Don't be in too much of hurry to call to find out the status of your press release. Remember that it takes time to sort, process and prepare most items for publication. Also, if an event is several weeks away, it may be pigeonholed for publication at a future date. Call if it has been some time (more than a week or two) since the item was submitted and the event is timely, or if there is a critical correction that needs to be made in the original submission.

If an item is time-sensitive and an important date is getting close, you can make a call to deliver a quick reminder to the editor that the usefulness of the item will expire if not published soon. But remember that because of the nature of the news business there is often no guarantee that an item can be published on a specific date. Despite advance planning, many times editors don't even know the exact content of an edition until the last minute, and something may come up that will override their plans and good intentions.

• **Be patient.** This especially applies during busy times such as the end of the traditional school year. Community papers are often inundated by photos and news releases relating to scholarships, awards, honor rolls, graduations (everything from pre-school to medical school), and announcements of school system retirements. The weeks prior to holidays or major local events can also throw off a paper's timing. Something that may appear in the paper within a week could be bumped a few days or even an extra week or two. Work around those busy times if you can. If not, be prepared to wait a little longer.

• **Get a name.** When you call to discuss a news release or story idea, or when you come to the office in person, make a note of the name of the person you spoke with. Many times a caller will later say they talked to "somebody" at the paper who assured them their press release would get into the paper on a certain day or that a photographer would be at their hot-dog supper, but they can't remember exactly who gave such assurances. Often these unidentified people were not in a position to make those promises. With many staff shifts and people coming and going at a newspaper, it is sometimes tough to track down an employee when all you have is a vague clue like "It sounded like a young girl" rather than a name.

- **Leave a number.** Editors have the potential to talk to a lot of people in a few days' time. That's one of the reasons it is important always to include a phone number when leaving a message and requesting a return call. Too often someone will tell the receptionist, "Just tell him I called. He's got my number." That may be so, but it also may be on one of those scraps of paper now two or three layers below the accumulated items on his desk. There may also be times when others are delegated to return calls and they don't have the caller's number.

- **Keep it short**. Even when an editor isn't fighting a deadline, he often has a full desk of work waiting to be done. That doesn't leave a lot of time for long telephone conversations. Callers who show some respect for an editor's busy schedule can win the undying gratitude of the news chief and may find that staffers are much more likely to promptly return phone messages left by them.

- **Be nice**. Many editors have a bad habit of automatically becoming defensive when they answer a phone call and hear screaming at the other end of the line. No matter what an editor, a reporter, or the newspaper is alleged to have done, directing emotional outbursts or insults at them is rarely an effective way to win them over to your side. Motivational speaker and writer Dale Carnegie said it best more than 60 years ago in his book *How to Win Friends & Influence People:* "The resentment that criticism engenders can demoralize employees, family members and friends, and still not correct the situation that has been condemned."

Here are two examples of typical calls. Which complaint do you think will be better received and acted upon?

"Yeah, this is a subscriber (or advertiser) to your newspaper, and I have a complaint. Why don't you ever get anything right down there? The other day I saw where you left my nephew's name out of the honor roll list. I can't tell you exactly where and when, but I see a lot of mistakes and I don't like it one bit. I'm gonna cancel my subscription (or advertising contract) and tell all my friends to do so."

"Hi, my name's Bob Smith. I enjoy reading your paper, but there's something that's bothering me. There was an article in Thursday about a little girl at our church who got a community service award, and it didn't have her mother's name spelled right. I know you guys have a lot to keep up with down there. This may not seem like a big thing, but I know her mom was disappointed. I was hoping you could run a corrected article."

It's understandable that when people are upset they will direct their anger or frustration at the offending party. But, believe me, an editor or reporter who is treated with a little kindness and respect by a caller who is explaining a problem is likely do all he or she can to resolve the problem. In fact, they will be more motivated to do so than after being threatened and berated.

- **Make an appointment.** People who assume that newspaper reporters and photographers are just sitting around the office waiting for a hot story to break must also believe that an editor hasn't much to do but wait for people to drop in for unexpected visits. That's not the case. Someone who would not dream of making unscheduled visits to doctors, lawyers or other professional offices do not think twice about dropping in to see a newspaper editor. While it is true that editors are not performing surgery or taking depositions, they do have important responsibilities and duties that may be interrupted by unplanned visits. Sometimes they can break away for these impromptu meetings and are happy to do so, but it is easier to plan the time if people call in advance. It also can keep visitors from having to wait in the lobby for someone to break free.

- **Call before faxing.** If in doubt about whether to send a fax, call ahead and ask. Most editors would rather spend a minute on the phone than go through a stack of unsolicited and useless faxes. Also, a call gives an editor notice that something of interest is coming. If the item is of no interest or use to the paper's readers, the call has saved both the editor and the sender time and effort. The same advice applies to e-mails.

• **Give advance notice for coverage requests.** Although the organizers of the Sweet Pickle Festival may have been planning their event for months, it sometimes occurs to them only the morning of the Miss Pickle Queen pageant to call the newspaper to request coverage.

Yes, newsrooms are set up to cover news stories quickly, but, for budgetary reasons, judgments must be made about when to scramble the news staff for breaking stories. It is a lot easier to plan and assign coverage to an event in advance than to account for overtime that was paid to cover the event at the last minute. Editors get enough surprises on a typical news day without having last-minute assignments added as a result of poor planning.

• **Don't demand that releases remain unchanged.** The opposite of giving too much latitude to the editor is not giving enough. To ask an editor not to edit is ill advised. An editor's job is to edit. Besides, one of the editor's responsibilities is to make sure every piece is consistent with the policies and tone of the paper.

A press release from a representative of an out-of-town company planning to build a hotel in our city illustrated this point. The cover sheet of the fax noted: "Please do not change the article. We would like it to run as written." But if that had been done the paper would have erroneously reported the location of the construction site and included at least one misspelled word.

Even editors need editing. I hired a consultant to edit this book. Like mosquitoes, editors may be annoying, but they do have a purpose in the grand scheme of life.

- **Don't make comparisons.** Many newspapers share common traits, but every newspaper has its own policies, schedules and priorities that may differ from other publications. One paper, for example, allows friends of the family to be listed as survivors in obituaries while another doesn't. When I worked for a small weekly in Central Florida, I had one loyal reader who always asked why our newspaper didn't do things the way the *Washington Post* did. I thought the reasons would be obvious—we didn't have the same staffing, resources, readers and we had a completely different coverage area and news focus.

Newspaper policies are put into place to maintain consistency and try to ensure fairness in meeting the needs of the readership. Once an exception is allowed, a precedent is set. Consistency is then more difficult to maintain. It never fails that someone will call after one exception is made—sometimes years after—and cite that one isolated example in arguing their case for similar treatment.

This is not to say that the way newspapers do things shouldn't be questioned—because they should—or that editors aren't ever interested in new ideas—because they are. And policies do need to be reviewed and updated from time to time to make sure the underlying reasons for them still make sense and that the newspaper is serving its readers.

But continuing to argue with an editor for an exception to a well-established and justified rule often ends up as a frustrating experience for everyone involved. A lifestyles editor once noted that the most heated complaint he ever received involved a woman who made it very obvious that she didn't agree with the paper's policy on publishing only the bride-elect's photo in engagement announcements. The editor explained the reason for the policy, which was so that the page design and allotted space could accommodate all the announcements. The caller still didn't agree and in retaliation threatened to withhold her wedding announcement from free publication in the newspaper. She eventually accepted the policy.

5. NEWSPAPER STYLE

"Spontaneous me," sang Whitman, and, in his innocence, let loose the hordes of uninspired scribblers who would one day confuse spontaneity with genius.

E.B. White .
Co-author
"The Elements of Style"
1979

Editors don't expect the same type of copy from news release writers as they do from the paper's full-time staff reporters, but are delighted when that does happen. People who regularly submit releases should read and become familiar with the style of the newspaper. Putting a release in that form increases the chances of publication and the potential that the published piece will be closer to what was originally submitted.

While newspapers differ in style in some respects, owing to their traditions, mission statements and the values of the communities they serve, there are some generally accepted standards to which most adhere. The following are a few tips that will make sure your news releases are always in style.

• **Addresses.** Do not abbreviate the words street, avenue and boulevard unless they follow a numbered address. Example: *The event will be held at 22 Twain Ave. The event will be held on Twain Avenue.*

• **a.m. and p.m.** For times of the day, use these abbreviations in lower case and with periods. It is redundant to write *"10 p.m. tonight"* or *"12 p.m. noon"* because p.m. and tonight mean the same thing, as do 12 p.m. and noon. It is less confusing to use the word *"noon"* instead of 12 p.m. and *"midnight"* instead of 12 a.m. Eliminate the 00s when writing times that are on the hour. Example: 8 p.m., not 8:00 p.m.

• **Dates.** Use Arabic numerical figures and don't follow the number with st, nd, rd or th as the dates are pronounced in speaking. Example: April 1, 2002; not April 1st, 2002. For the month abbreviate Jan., Feb., Aug., Sept., Oct., Nov. and Dec., but spell out March, April, May, June and July. Spell out all months when not using the full date. Example: The event will be held in January. The event will be held on Jan. 7.

• **Datelines.** Capitalize the name of the city from which the news release or story originates. The state abbreviation is usually not necessary for local releases. Papers may not use datelines on the news releases they publish, but including datelines on a release can be useful to show the editor right away that the item involves local news.

• **Days of the week.** Do not abbreviate Sunday, Monday, Tuesday, Wednesday, Thursday, Friday, and Saturday.

• **Names.** Don't use first names after the first reference unless there is more than one person with the same last name and distinguishing between them would be confusing. Example: "Bob Jones will be honored on Jan. 14. Jones has achieved 50 years of perfect attendance in the Rotary Club." Some newspapers such as *The Wall Street Journal* use courtesy titles such as Mr., Mrs. and Ms. before the last name of a person. A title, however, is no substitute for a first name on a first reference. For example, "Mrs. Robinson's third-grade class toured the Bubble Gum Museum on Thursday," should have noted the teacher's first name if this is the first time she is mentioned in the story or photo caption. When a person is well known by a nickname still use the full formal name in the first reference and use quote marks to designate the nickname. Example: Senator Henry M. "Scoop" Jackson.

• **Numbers.** Spell out one through nine. Use figures for 10 and above. Example: The club will honor eight members who have 15 years of service. Exceptions include dates, weights, ages and percentages. Example: "On July 17, 8-year-old Bobby Jones hooked a 9 pound 7 ounce bass, which was 10 percent bigger than the next largest fish caught that day." (This is one area where newspaper style differs from what is generally used in other periodicals and books. *The Chicago Manual of Style* advises in most writing to spell out whole numbers one through 100 when they appear in ordinary text.)

• **OK.** Do not use "*okay.*" Other forms are OK'd, OK'ing, and OKs. Example: "The City Council OK'd the parade route."

• **Political parties.** Capitalize references to parties. Example: "All local Democrats are invited to the Democratic Party meeting."

• **Pronouns.** Do not use *they* or *their* with a collective noun such as a single organization. This misuse is so common in speech that even seasoned writers can make the mistake. Example: "The City Council approved *its* budget." Not, "The City Council approved *their* budget." As one board or group, the Council is a singular noun. It is, however, correct to write: "The City Council's members approved their budget." In that case the plural noun "members" agrees with the plural pronoun "their."

• **Room numbers.** Capitalize the word "Room" and use figures to designate a location. Example: The meeting will be held in Room 3 at the community college.

• **Seasons.** Do not capitalize spring, summer, fall (autumn) and winter unless they begin a sentence or are part of a formal name. Example: The annual Ourtown Spring Festival was held so late this year it was almost summer by the time it opened.

• **Slang.** In general, avoid the use of slang until after the use becomes widely accepted. Some expressions such as computer *hacker* have quickly gained such acceptance.

• **States.** Spell out state names when they are mentioned by themselves. Example: "The group will travel to Tennessee on Jan. 7." Abbreviate most names when used with a city. Example: "The group will travel to Nashville, Tenn. on Jan. 7." Eight states do not have prose abbreviations. Write out the following state names: Alaska, Hawaii, Idaho, Iowa, Maine, Ohio, Texas and Utah.

The common abbreviations used by newspapers for states are: Ala., Ariz., Calif., Colo., Conn., Del., Fla., Ga., Ill., Ind., Kan., Ky., La., Md., Mass., Mich., Minn., Miss., Mo., Mont., Neb., Nev., N.H., N.J., N.Y., N.C., N.D., Okla., Ore., Pa., P.R. (Puerto Rico), R.I., S.C., S.D., Tenn., Vt., Va., Wash., W.Va., Wis., Wyo.

Use the U.S. Postal Service's two-letter ZIP code abbreviations for the states when including addresses in news releases. They are: AL (Alabama), AK (Alaska), AZ (Arizona), AR (Arkansas), CA (California), CO (Colorado), CT (Connecticut), DE (Delaware), DC (District of

Columbia), FL (Florida), GA (Georgia), HI (Hawaii), ID (Idaho), IL (Illinois), IN (Indiana), IA (Iowa), KS (Kansas), KY (Kentucky), LA (Louisiana), ME (Maine), MD (Maryland), MA (Massachusetts), MI (Michigan), MN (Minnesota), MS Mississippi), MO (Missouri), MT (Montana), NE (Nebraska), NV (Nevada), NH (New Hampshire), NJ (New Jersey), NM (New Mexico), NY (New York), NC (North Carolina), ND (North Dakota), OH (Ohio), OK (Oklahoma), OR (Oregon), PA Pennsylvania), PR (Puerto Rico), RI (Rhode Island), SC (South Carolina), SD (South Dakota), TN (Tennessee), TX (Texas), UT (Utah), VT (Vermont), VA (Virginia), WA (Washington), WV (West Virginia), WI (Wisconsin), WY (Wyoming).

- **Trademarks.** Newspapers that publish the names of brand-name products without the proper capitalization often receive notifications from the trademark holder. Be sure that such names in press releases are properly used. Examples: Weedeater, Kleenex, Mace, Popsicle, Windbreaker, Xerox, GORE-TEX, Wite-Out, Weight Watchers, ROLLERBLADE, and Velcro.

- **Years.** Use figures when writing years, even at the beginning of a sentence. Example: 1956 was my favorite year. Use an s without an apostrophe when writing decades or centuries. Example: The 1960s, not the 1960's. The '60s, not the '60's.

6. FINDING THE ANGLE

A word has power in and of itself.
It comes from nothing into sound and
meaning; it gives origin to all things.
By means of the word can a man deal
with the world on equal terms? And
the word is sacred.

N. Scott Momaday
Writer
1969

If you want your press release or feature article to catch a newspaper editor's eye and engage his or her interest, it is a good idea to approach your subject in an original or unusual way. This is referred to as a "news hook," because its intent is to *hook* the reader's interest.

Editors are used to seeing the basic who, what, where, when, etc., etc. and it's important for that information to be there. But how you arrange those facts may make a difference in the kind of attention your submission receives and the kind of play it gets in print. The difference involves what is called the "angle," and it is exactly what newspaper reporters do to make their stories more readable, interesting, and likely to hold the reader's attention than a bland recitation of the facts as they occurred. The angle of the release should not affect the accuracy or clarity of the report, but it should enhance it and make it either more appealing or understandable to the reader.

Here's an example:

> The last PTO meeting of Davenport Elementary School will be held Thursday night, May 30, at 7 p.m.
>
> All parents are invited to the meeting where the program will feature a Physical Education demonstration as well as closing ceremonies from this week's field day competition, honoring all the winners.

Here's how the release could have been written with a different angle:

> Winners from this week's field day competition will be honored Thursday night during Davenport Elementary School's last PTO meeting of the year.
>
> Besides the field day closing ceremonies, a physical education demonstration will be a part of the meeting program. All parents are invited to attend the May 30 meeting that begins a 7:30 p.m.

The same information is included, it is just arranged in a different way. The release is correct either way, but it just might appeal more to the editor and to readers in the latter form. What can be tricky is that there is not only one angle or a correct angle for every release or story. There are often several ways to approach it, and each writer can apply his or her own talents and ideas to the task.

There are, however, a few common methods that may help in finding an angle. Here are some of them:

• **Stress the most important point.** Often a writer wants to publicize an important aspect of an event or meeting but winds up burying that information under more mundane facts about the time and place and organization involved. If the item central to the release is important, try to mention it as early as possible—in the first sentence or even in the first word. In the example I used, the honoring of the winners of the field day was emphasized. I could have just as easily started with the physical education demonstration, which also may have been of interest to many people. But I always figure that children getting some public recognition will attract the most interest from parents of the youngsters as well as the students themselves.

• **Personalize it.** People like to read about other people and how they react to or are affected by issues, rather than the dry issues themselves. A news release about a fund-raising walk for cancer victims can attract much more interest if a survivor's own compelling story is told. Putting a human face on a topic helps the reader identify with those involved in the story.

• **Emphasize the unusual.** Is there anything different about this event or item that sets it apart from most others? Readers may be used to seeing the monthly notice of the Chamber of Commerce meeting, but they would be intrigued to read that this month's meeting is being held in a clover field where a program on African Killer Bees will be presented by the local beekeepers association. That's much different from discussing your normal agenda around a conference room table and should be pointed out right away in any press release issued about the upcoming meeting.

• **Find the irony.** A lead sentence that starts with the word "although" can catch the readers' attention by tipping them off that there will be some kind of twist coming up. For example, a release announcing that the mayor will be judging the Women's Club macaroni marathon might begin:

> Although Mayor Bob Jones spends much of his time deciding how to manage the city government's bureaucracy, he will be spending Tuesday night trying to determine who has the tastiest sauce and pasta.

• **Expose the conflict.** This angle may be perceived as "going negative," but the grim reality is that conflict is often news. A press release that involves a health or safety concern or public issue dispute will attract media attention.

• **Play to the reader's emotions.** Most people want to contribute toward a good cause, but there are so many pitches being made these days that we have all had to become more selective about where we commit our time, talents and money. Often releases come across an editor's desk about benefit yard sales, bake sales or concerts that don't disclose who is benefiting or why such an effort is needed. Some writers may assume that most people in the community know the personal tragedies involved if they just write, "The proceeds from this sale will benefit the Jay Robinson family." Appeals are more effective when details are revealed.

For example, mentioning that the benefit is being held to help a child suffering from leukemia or a family whose home has been destroyed by fire can induce more people to pay attention to the article and respond to it. The sooner the reason for the benefit is mentioned, the sooner that interest is engaged and acted upon.

- **Tie into a current event or issue of local or national interest.** Announcing that a local judge or district attorney will speak at the next Kiwanis Club meeting could take on added interest if the subject of that official's talk happens to deal with issues of public interest. The program may involve the judge's thoughts on a high profile trial (a celebrity murder case perhaps), for example, or a controversial Supreme Court ruling (on topics such as abortion or immigration).

- **Update old releases.** Often people want the same news item to be published more than once, especially about an upcoming meeting or event. But a newspaper's policy may be to run each submitted item only once. This makes sense when you consider that there are so many new releases coming in and a finite amount of space available in the newspaper. Update the release so that a reprinting is justified. It may be a case of simply changing the leading paragraph to emphasize a different aspect of the event or meeting.

An example would be starting off with the fact that a dunking booth is part of the fall festival activities in the new release when that particular activity had been listed with others down in the third paragraph in the initial release. Adding something entirely new to the release can be an even better way to justify additional play. For instance, starting off with the announcement that a new act has been signed to perform at a previously publicized benefit concert.

- **Paint a picture in the reader's mind.** Yes, a press release should tell a story using nouns and verbs and leave out the fancy adjectives. But there is an exception to every rule. Sometimes a descriptive phrase can be an effective way to lead into a press release. For example:

> The smell of fried fish and buttered corn on the cob will fill the air during the annual Lions Club picnic on Friday, Oct. 31.

Just don't get too carried away setting the scene, however, that the point of the release gets hidden in the background.

• **Find the local tie-in.** A press release about an honor presented to a student in another county or state may not be of much interest to the readers of the *Local Weekly Tribune*. But readers may be interested if that the student is daughter or granddaughter of one of their neighbors or is a graduate of the local school system. Make sure that any local connection is prominently mentioned in the release. If you haven't already noticed, the operative word here is **local**.

• **Ask a question.** "Ever wonder where the money you give to the United Way ends up?" That could be a good way to begin a press release about an agency meeting of the local United Way or other nonprofit group. If you ask a question in an article, though, be sure to provide the answer or explain how the reader can find it.

7. WHAT'S NEWS?

Newspapers are unable, seemingly,
to discriminate between a bicycle acci-
dent and the collapse of civilization.

George Bernard Shaw
Playwright
1931

Our newsroom had a semi-serious rule of thumb as to how we set our news priorities. The story that got the most attention was the auto accident the publisher saw on her way to work.

Although suggestions from the boss may get the attention of the news staff for obvious reasons, all story tips have to go through a complex and subjective consideration process to determine the extent of newspaper resources committed to coverage. Exactly what that process is, though, is difficult to define. That's because it varies from newspaper to newspaper and editor to editor. And sometimes, even from day to day. Look at any newspapers published the same day from different areas. Some may agree on the top national or foreign story but others won't, and local news stories will often dominate the page. A car wreck in the town in which the paper is published may get better play than a plane crash overseas, and justifiably so. These stories can beat out the big wire service news because they relate things that are close to home and nearer to the hearts of the paper's readers.

Somebody has to be responsible for filtering and prioritizing all the millions of bits of information that are out there. In most cases it is the editor who decides what is important to a significant portion of the paper's readers. An editor's news judgment involves managing people, money and resources, as well as filling news space. But decisions on what to cover and how to treat stories do not stop with the editors who are responsible for what goes on the printed page. Reporters themselves have a lot of discretion over what they cover on their beats as well as how their assignments are developed and completed.

Timeliness is always a consideration. A press release about a local business that changed ownership last week is news. If the same thing happened several months ago it's not—that's history.

Timing can also be a factor in another way. The story is told about an New England editor who was strapped for a piece on deadline when the lead article he had planned for the next day's paper fell through. He supposedly made the snap decision to fill the space with a report of an alleged gang rape in a poolroom. Up until then, the article had been relegated to the police roundup on an inside page. The prominently placed story got national attention, eventually catching the interest of the moviemakers in Hollywood and resulting in an Academy Award for Jodie Foster, the lead in "The Accused." This is one of several cases where changes in circumstances produce huge swings in news value and story placement.

Many excellent story ideas, however, come from the public. *The Pensacola News-Journal* puts it this way, "...if it's happening and it's important to you or to someone else in the community, it's news." But it is up to the newspaper editors to determine how much of that "news" is reported. Most people have a good idea of what constitutes news in their community, sometimes a better idea than their own hometown newspaper editors. There are times when proud parents believe their child's second birthday should outweigh in news value the city council's outlawing the practice of religion within the municipal boundaries, but that is not usually the case. People know what they and other readers in their area will find interesting and—as customers of the local printed news service—what they want to see in their newspaper. Consider the following:

> Two phone calls in different parts of the country told the same sad news of a young man's death. To one family the call brought enormous grief, and to another a great deal of hope.
>
> Alan Smith had been waiting six weeks for such a call. As he hurriedly packed for his trip to the hospital in North Carolina he had little time to ponder the fate of the 20-year-old Vermont man who had died and who would remain unknown to him. Smith only knew that a compatible kidney had finally been found that could save his life.

That story was the result of a phone call from a friend of the Smith family who thought a tip about a local man undergoing an organ transplant might be an interesting human interest story and wondered whether the local newspaper thought it was good enough to share with our readers.

It was.

Requesting coverage

If you want newspaper coverage of an event, simply call the paper's editor and ask for it. That doesn't guarantee that a newspaper will respond by sending a reporter or photographer or both, but it increases the chances of getting that publicity several times over. Too many times, people will call after the fact to complain about the lack of coverage of an event that they incorrectly assumed the paper had known about.

Community newspaper staffers pride themselves on knowing what is going on in their coverage areas, but nobody can know everything that's happening or about to happen. Editors can't read minds, and just because an annual event was covered last year doesn't mean it is automatically scheduled for coverage this time around. Even if a release on an upcoming local event has been published, a request should be made if coverage is wanted or expected. And remember, don't wait until the last minute to make that request. Call ahead at least a week in advance of the event.

Even with advance notice and a request, newspapers can't afford to have staff members attend every seminar, meeting or workshop being held in a town or county. That's why it is important when making such requests to mention unusual aspects of the meeting or subjects that would be of interest to a large number of the paper's readers.

Weekend events may be particularly difficult to cover for small, non-daily papers that may have fewer staff members available on Saturday and Sunday. They may have to change schedules or pay overtime to cover events outside the usual workweek. In such cases, event organizers should suggest that advance stories be done on the upcoming event. By getting the coverage before the event, organizers may be able to increase attendance, and then follow up with a press release to report what happened.

Organizers who have flexibility as to the scheduling of an event and who want to increase the chances of getting the local newspaper to cover it, should seek a day with the fewest potential conflicts. Some weekday evenings during particular times of the month may be busy for newspaper staff members due to local government meetings or other regularly scheduled activities that draw media attention. Many city councils and other local boards meet early in the week, on Monday and Tuesday nights, while churches often schedule meetings for Wednesday. Your best chance of attracting a news reporter or photographer to an event is to plan it for a slow news day or night. Even the Pope's historic visit to Cuba in 1998 couldn't compete with reports of a sex scandal at the White House. It doesn't make sense to try to compete for news coverage with another news event if you don't have to.

Some government officials or business leaders are inclined to call a "news conference" to announce items that would be better communicated through a release. Press conferences should be used only when there is some important news to break to a large group of media at one time, such as the announcement that the city has landed a new NFL franchise or a major industry. Remember the story of the boy who cried wolf once too often. Too many conferences called for routine announcements can eventually result in a lack of interest and attendance by the media at such staged events.

That's not news

In addition to coverage requests, editors sometimes receive calls from people trying to downplay the significance of an incident they don't think is worth mentioning in the newspaper. Just because this particular incident happens to reflect badly on them doesn't affect their opinion of what is news—or so they usually say.

Of all the items published in a local newspaper, the police reports often draw the most controversy and anguish for editors. Understandably, people don't like their names, or those of family and friends, appearing in a negative light. About 95 of 100 libel claims resulting from alleged injury to reputation come from publication of charges of crime, immorality, incompetence or inefficiency, according to the Associated Press.

The point can be made that in our judicial system a person is presumed to be innocent until proven guilty, but when an arrest is reported in the newspaper, the suspect has already been convicted in the minds of the readers. Still, newspapers have a duty to report such things because most people are interested in knowing that a neighbor has been arrested for burglary or selling illegal drugs. If newspapers were to wait until after a trial or plea bargain before reporting on a crime it could be several months before this information would be provided to the readers.

Much has been made about how pre-trial publicity can interfere with a fair trial by prejudicing the jury, but publication of crime information can also directly benefit the process. Dissemination of the facts in a case may draw out new witnesses of whom neither the prosecution nor defense had been aware. Reporting arrests also helps keep readers informed of how their police agencies are operating. If law enforcement officers are not making many arrests, the citizens need to know. If they are making too many unreasonable arrests, people need to know that as well.

In most cases, newspaper police reports are public records available to be viewed by anyone. Only the fact that newspapers and other news media can widely distribute that information makes them the target of requests to suppress reports. Everyone seems to have a good reason why his drunk driving arrest should not be newsworthy. But if a newspaper wants to maintain its credibility with readers, no exceptions can be made in reporting arrests.

One reported incident involved an apparent love triangle in which a man broke into a couple's apartment, stabbed the husband and assaulted the wife. The newspaper editor didn't hear from the assault suspect, but did get a few calls from his mother. She said her son wasn't a bad kid and that he could lose his job because of the paper's report. She noted that she wasn't so concerned about the breaking and entering charge, the stabbing and the indication that her son was having an affair with a married woman, but was upset about the allegation that he had assaulted the woman.

"My son would never do that," she said. "He loves her."

That kind of love is news.

In another case, it was reported that a woman had allegedly stabbed her husband. She called to complain that the report left the impression that both she and her husband had been drinking when the incident occurred. She wanted to make it clear that she was sober when she stabbed him.

It is often hard to explain to those who are personally involved the necessity for objective reporting. The strong emotions that lead to incidents and are publicly revealed in crime reports are also the human feelings that make a news story compelling to readers.

In another case two elderly neighbors had been carrying on a feud about the location of their common property line. The heated arguing escalated until one day it resulted in a physical confrontation and one of the men died of a heart attack. A relative of the dead man called the paper and said he was upset about the coverage, but not as upset as the dead man's stepson would be. The stepson was in the military and was being called back from overseas for the funeral. "I don't think we'll be able to control him." In this case, the implied threat was never acted upon.

Victims of crime are sometimes the ones who call to request that police reports not be published. Because there are often compelling reasons to protect a victim's rights in addition to those of the accused, some editors will consider the circumstances and make exceptions to the usual reporting policies. Although such exceptions may be rare, editors want to be fair, so it doesn't hurt for the victim or defendant to call and plead their cases. If nothing else, they can add some detail to the police report that could help justify or explain to readers why an incident occurred, factors the law calls mitigating circumstances, and which may not be detailed in the written report.

Also, if the charge is eventually dismissed or the suspect is judged innocent at trial, that should be reported to the paper so that it can be publicized. Reporters usually don't have the time to follow up on every arrest report, unless the trial itself becomes big news. That leaves it up to the accused to make sure the outcome is reported. This often doesn't happen, however, because many people who are charged but later acquitted don't want the incident and their involvement in it called to the readers' attention again.

People should keep crime reports in perspective. Nobody likes to look bad in front of the whole community, but people often understand about transgressions, and news reports fade from the public consciousness over time. Some excerpts from one letter to the editor sum it up.

> When I was 17, I "borrowed" three gallons of gas from a local business. I was with three of my friends and in my car. We all had money in our pockets to buy gas, but it was more "fun" this way. We got caught by the police and it was no longer funny.
>
> Afterwards, I did find a few parents were not sure they wanted their son to pal around with me and a few parents were not too sure they wanted their daughter to date me. I knew I was being watched to see what kind of a person I would become and I tried to make the most of my time.
>
> It passed in a short period of time….I'm not proud of what I did, I made a mistake, but I hope I learned from it.

Maybe others can learn from such experiences too, but they have to be made aware of them first.

8. Photo-ops

(The media) are a pest,
by the very nature of that
camera in (their) hands.

Princess Anne
British royal
1986

A picture is said to be worth a thousand words. From experience, I can tell you that it is a lot less work to click that shutter than to type those words.

What a camera can record in a thousandth of a second can take up the same space in a newspaper that would require a reporter hours to fill with type. Former *Avon Park (Fla.) Sun* editor Jack Stroud used to acknowledge this by referring to the three Fs—Film Fills Fast. But photos and other art elements do much more than take up space. They help make gray newspaper pages come alive and consequently more attractive to readers. Most people won't read every story in a newspaper, but their eyes will usually scan every photograph, even if only for a second.

That is what makes photos a valuable asset to a newspaper editor who is challenged daily or weekly to make the best use of available space. At times, a photo spread can often provide better coverage of an event than a 500-word feature story.

But even if newspapers have one or more full-time photographers on staff, don't expect editors to send one running every time you call. No matter how dependent an editor may be on art, not every activity justifies a photo assignment. With a little planning and imagination, however, many events can qualify as a bone fide photo opportunity or as it is known in the world of media, a "photo-op."

Again, the best way to get what you want is to ease the burden of effort at the editor's end. People often call to request a photo of, say, a business seminar or guest speaker and leave it up to the photographer to come up with an angle or perspective that makes for an interesting photo. But having already taken hundreds of photos of business seminars and guest speakers, he may be running out of fresh ideas. Even if the photographer is brilliant, energetic and bursting with creativity, the photo assignment may not even get to him because of an unenthused editor who is hearing the same request for the hundredth time. It is usually the editor, not the staff photographer, you should call with your photo request. While photographers may take ideas from the public about what to shoot, assignments from the editors who plan the paper take priority.

You not only have to make the request; you have to sell your idea to the editor for a new and different photo. There are several possible approaches:

• **End result.** Just as the first paragraph, or lead, of a news release should get to the point about the purpose of the article, a photo about a fund-raising event should show, when possible, the desired result of the activity. If the activity to be promoted is a new truck for the volunteer fire department, have some firefighters climb on a fire truck (the new model or the old broken-down one) or pose near an empty bay at the fire station.

One of the biggest wastes of film is the dreaded check passing shot. It is also known in the trade as the "grip and grin" because it usually involves two or more people smiling and shaking hands as a check is handed over. Such an image often says nothing about the activity for which the funds were raised or donated. Because of its lack of visual appeal, readers may be tempted to skip the caption and never learn what the photo op was all about. Using a prop such as an oversized check shows a little more planning and imagination. At least with this enhancement the reader can see what is written on the mock check, whereas in a typical check passing shot the unidentifiable item being passed might as well be a blank piece of paper (which it sometimes is if the actual check is not available in time for the photo.)

Another way around this is to substitute cold hard cash for the check. An idea one publisher came up with when he was faced with a check-passing photo request led the local art league, recipient of the donation, to request that the bank donating the large sum of money provide a stack of bills. A photo of the art league director fanning these large denominations certainly made for a more unusual and interesting donation picture than the typical grip and grin shot.

Many newspapers also set a minimum limit on the donation amount so that everyone who regularly donates a few bucks to a favorite cause doesn't get his photo in the paper every other day. That limit could be set at $100 or $5,000, depending on the generosity of donors in the area. Getting an exception to those limits may depend on a creative staging of the photo-op.

• **Props**. Using colorful, large or unusual props that relate to the purpose of the photo can add a fresh angle. But just as a check is a photo cliché, a banner or sign can be just as bad.

Every year, a chamber of commerce would promote its Lobster Fest event by having its director and staff unfurl a banner that essentially said "Annual Lobster Fest," and included the time and date of the event. That didn't leave much information to include in a photo caption and it certainly did not hold much interest to the reader. One year a newspaper editor decided to include a different prop, the obvious one—lobster. There were some logistical problems at first. Because the lobsters had to be fresh, live animals were to be flown in just before the event, which meant one of the Fest's lobsters couldn't be used for an advance photo. Chamber officials solved that with the cooperation of a local grocer who agreed to lend a few live lobsters in exchange for a mention in the caption. The result was a livelier photo shoot and an attention-grabbing photograph.

- **Show activity**. An unposed natural photo of people doing something is always more interesting than people who look like they are standing around waiting to have their picture taken. One of the purposes of a news photo is to tell a story, and one of the best ways to tell something is to show it. Ask yourself, "What is the purpose of having this picture published in the newspaper?" Then determine the best way to convey that purpose through an image.

- **Holiday tie-in.** This angle also takes planning. Newspapers by their very nature try to be timely and often seek out photos and stories that relate to the current season or time of year. A photo idea that relates to an upcoming holiday or season can often catch an editor's attention.

The publicity person for a local Girl Scout troop effectively used this technique when she called about a father-daughter campout scheduled for the weekend before Father's Day. She suggested that a photo from the event might be appropriate for the newspaper's upcoming edition on or before the day designated to honor fatherhood. The key word is "upcoming" because photo assignments take time to schedule and the photos time to produce and prepare for publication. Calling the day before the holiday can be too late, and a holiday photo that is available a few days after the holiday is worthless. For dailies, figure on at least a week in advance of the holiday, and for weeklies about two weeks.

The holiday tie-in idea is not as appealing to editors for Halloween and Christmas, which are times when newspapers usually have an abundance of photo requests.

Submitting photos

No matter how well you pitch a photo opportunity to an editor there will be times when a staff photographer just won't be available to cover your event. That's when you should take matters into your own hands.

Newspapers, especially smaller ones, usually are more than happy to accept photos submitted by the public. Sometimes they're even willing to pay for them. But don't expect the same payoffs from the traditional press that are handed out by national tabloids. Yes, there are some publications that will pay $200 to $300 for an exclusive spot news shot of a terrible accident or reclusive celebrity. But most of the time shutterbugs will be lucky to get $5 or $10 a photo, and in many cases you may do well just to get a photo credit for your efforts along with the publicity you hoped for in the first place.

Too often people are reluctant to volunteer their own photo services because of the difficulty finding black and white film or because they don't have an expensive 35 mm camera. Neither, however, should be a concern. Because newspapers print a lot of black and white photos, especially on inside pages, people assume they must only use black and white film, and it is true that many papers prefer black and white prints because they produce a better image on their equipment. However, a large number of newspapers are now shooting color exclusively, even though the majority of photos come out in black and white when they are published. Most of the photographs transmitted by the Associated Press wire service, in fact, are in color, although most of them end up being reproduced in grayscale on the inside pages of newspapers.

A color print or negative that is in focus and shows the subject in adequate lighting is usually all that is needed for producing an acceptable image in the paper. Many newspapers use electronic darkrooms, which can help improve the transfer of images from the original photos to the printed page through digital imaging. What can't be used, at least without much success, are images clipped from other newspapers or magazines.

Besides the obvious copyright infringement concerns, the print quality of a third or fourth generation copy is just not going to be acceptable.

Many newspapers also accept images from digital cameras. Those images, however, should be taken at a high enough resolution so that they can be adequately reproduced. While many digital photos may look sharp on a computer screen at 72 pixels per inch—or dots per inch (dpi)—that same picture won't look as good when printed. For comparison purposes, a color film negative is about 1,000 dpi. The images, at least 1600 x 1200 pixels, should be transferred to a floppy disk and saved as tiff or jpeg files. Don't bring in a camera and expect the paper to download photos while you wait. Some papers will also accept digital images by e-mail, but be sure to check with the photo editor first to see how he prefers these files to be transferred. Unlike text files, images take up a lot more memory and newspaper webmasters don't appreciate having their e-mail boxes jammed up by huge data transfers. Do not print your digital image to your paper printer and assume that it can be used in that form by the newspaper. A paper copy, however, can be helpful in showing what the image looks like. Include the digital image on a disc along with the paper copy or a Web site address that tells where a high-resolution file can be found for downloading. The closer you can get to the original, whether it be the digital image or film negative, the better the final reproduction will be on the newsprint.

While an expensive professional 35mm camera body and lens or a state-of-the art digital image recorder may increase the chances of getting a good, sharp photograph, all photographers should remember that the most important piece of equipment is the human eye that recognizes that a good photo exists. After that, the camera is merely a recorder of what the eye has seen. Photographers can increase their chances of having their photos used and getting good play in the paper by following a few simple rules.

• **Fill the frame.** Space is a terrible thing to waste, especially considering the high cost of newsprint. A pitfall of many photographers is to be timid and shoot from too far away. Trying to be inconspicuous during a ceremony or meeting, some people will stand at the back of the room to take a picture of the featured speaker or guest of honor who is far away in the front. What comes out is a photo showing a well-lit row of the backs of heads and a dark area where the subject of the picture was. Newspaper photographers who have the reputations of being aggressive—possibly to the point of being considered rude—are often the ones who consistently bring back the best pictures. They are not afraid to get close and fill the entire viewfinder of their camera with the subject they are photographing.

Edmond "Ed" Arnold, who is considered the father of modern newspaper design, had a great four-word rule when it came to photo editing, which should be also be considered when taking pictures. "Enlarge generously; crop ruthlessly." That sounds like a contradiction, but it isn't. What Arnold was saying is that when you have a good image, show it off by making it bigger. And when you have a weak photo cut it down in size, leaving only the best part. As far as submissions go, photo editors will cut most weak photos completely from consideration.

• **Close ranks.** A common problem with submitted photos are gaps between the subjects or items being photographed. When shooting a group, photographers need to take charge and pose people closely together, even if Charley doesn't particularly like Edith or Roy. When shooting an activity or news scene such control may not be possible, but a photographer may still be able to alter the angle and view to compress more into the frame and eliminate dead space. Unless subjects have strong feelings about how they want to be posed, most will defer to the photographer's wishes. And even if a person or group insists on a certain pose, the photographer should take other angles to give the editor a choice.

• **Limit the number of people in the photo**. Obviously, if the purpose of a photo is to show the size of the crowd that attended the downtown Bean Bag Festival, then the more the merrier. But in most cases newspapers prefer no more than four or five people in a photo. That way less caption space is needed to identify the people who are pictured and each person can be clearly identified. Because photos may have to be reduced in size to fit the page design, individual faces in a large group may be indistinguishable.

• **Avoid backlighting.** Too often a good shot of people is ruined because their faces are in a shadow. This problem can occur when the sun is behind the subject or when a building overhang or the bill of a cap is shading part or all of the face. While a newspaper's electronic darkroom can be used to lighten some areas of a photo, detail is often lost. A good way to avoid this is by shooting with your back to the sunlight. Harsh shadows can be avoided by shooting under some cloud cover or the shade of some tree branches that diffuse the sunlight. You can also use a photo flash unit—yes, even outdoors in the sunlight—to fill in shadows.

• **Avoid cluttered backgrounds.** When you're concentrating on focusing in on your subjects, sometimes you don't notice what's around them. In a two-dimensional photo of two people standing in front of a tree it can appear that branches are growing out of their heads like antlers. The contrast between the background and subjects should also be considered. People with light-colored clothing or complexions should generally be put in front of darker backdrops. Always be aware of everything that may appear in your photograph.

• **Take several exposures.** Good news photographers don't leave getting a good shot to chance. It is not uncommon for professionals to take an entire 36-exposure roll—or more than one roll—of one pose or angle to get a great picture.

Former editor Bill Dixon of the *Kissimmee (Fla.) Gazette* used to say, "Film is cheap." Of course, he didn't say that at budget time or when he was trying to control costs. What he meant was that taking two or three shots of a subject and having none of them meet the quality standards for publication is a waste of money in terms of time, effort and film. But taking a dozen or more and getting one good shot that can be printed is a bargain by comparison. Taking one or two exposures almost guarantees that at least one of the people in the photo will have her eyes closed or be wearing a funny facial expression between the time the shutter snaps open and closed. The more photos taken, the better the chances of a good picture developing.

• **Smile**. In his book *How To Win Friends & Influence People,* motivational speaker Dale Carnegie wrote, "Your smile is a messenger of your good will." Newspaper consultant Edward Henninger notes that if the subject of a newspaper photo is smiling, readers feel that person is more likeable. A frown, on the other hand, gives readers a negative impression.

• **Go for the unusual shape**. Even professional photographers can get into the rut of taking the same horizontal or vertical images. Though your rectangular camera viewfinder can't change, look for the photo that will give an editor something different. It may be a tall building or a long rubber hose gushing water at one end. In such cases, you may ignore the rule about filling the frame and allow the editor to crop the top or sides to come up with an unusual shape.

• **Photo print sizes**. Just as press releases should come on standard-sized sheets of paper to make them easier to handle, larger sized photos are desirable. Some papers require photos to be no smaller than 5 by 7 inches. Avoid turning in thumbnail-sized prints or small cutouts that can easily get lost.

• **Studio quality portraits.** Once a newspaper has a photo of a person on file—either in a folder in a file cabinet or stored in a digital format—it is often there to stay. It's a good idea to supply your own studio portrait if you plan to be in the news for some reason, such as a run for political office or other high-profile position. (Some newspapers may even subscribe to the motto "If you can't say anything bad about a person, at least use a bad picture of him.")

One county commissioner always complained that the file photo the local newspaper regularly used of him made him look like a criminal. It didn't help his case that the bald head and leering grin displayed in the photo bore an uncanny resemblance to characteristics made famous by Superman's archenemy Lex Luthor. Eventually the commissioner provided the newspaper with a studio portrait that projected a more law-abiding image.

Some papers will insist on using only their own photographer's shot, but many will gladly accept a studio print. Don't assume, however, that once a print is submitted the paper will use it forever. Many papers are reluctant to use a photo more than a year old, and some previously sub-mitted photos you may assume would still be on file may have been either discarded after their initial use or misfiled. It is best to send a fresh photo with each submission.

• **Photo captions**. Always attach caption—or cutline—information to the photo on a piece of paper taped to the back or the bottom of the print. Even though that information may already be on the accompanying press release, photos and releases are often separated during the process of preparing an item for publication. A photo without caption information is like most morning shift copy editors without their first cup of coffee—virtually useless. Many newspapers still have files containing old photos of people who were probably well known to former employees who saved the pictures years ago. But because their predecessors didn't bother to identify these subjects, the photos are of little use to current staff members.

A good caption, or cutline, should answer the basics of who, what, when, where, how and why. Also remember what the Associated Press style manual calls "the Cardinal Rule" that should never be violated: Don't write a caption without first seeing the picture. That may seem obvious, but there are times when people will turn in a roll of film and write out a description of what they think the picture will show before seeing what actually came out. This can result in misidentification of people in the picture and sometimes even a different interpretation of the events. More than once, a newspaper photo has shown a convict being escorted from a courtroom by a plainclothes policeman with a caption that has erroneously turned the cop into the criminal. Standard procedure is to identify subjects from left to right.

Print the headline from the news release, contact name and daytime phone number on the caption information sheet. Avoid writing on the back of the photo because the ink or impression of the pen may show through.

• **Getting credit.** If you want recognition for taking the photo you have submitted, ask for it by including a credit line. Submissions that don't identify the photographer end up being listed only as "courtesy photos."

• **Returning photos.** Some newspapers have a policy of not returning unsolicited photos, but others will. Find out the policy before submitting an irreplaceable photo. To increase the chances of getting back your photo, include a self-addressed stamped envelope or a note asking for the photo to be left at the newspaper's reception desk for pickup after publication.

Some papers set up a box or file accessible to the public where "courtesy" photos are placed after they have been published. In many cases, however, those photos remain unclaimed, even by those who insisted at the time of submission that they wanted to retrieve the photo. Don't expect the paper to keep the photo forever, even those that are stored digitally, because computer memory and file space are often in high demand. *The Pensacola (Fla.) News-Journal,* for example, will only keep photos on file for three months.

• **Ordering news photos**. While the sale of photos is not the primary business of a newspaper, such services have become an opportunity for papers to generate additional revenue. Sometimes the photographers will do it themselves as a sideline. Call the photo department of the newspaper to find out the reprint policy of your local paper.

9. Dealing with Reporters

*A news-writer is a man
without virtue, who lies at
home for his own profit.*

Samuel Johnson
English essayist
1758

If you make your story angle compelling enough to catch an editor's imagination you may end up having your press release turned into a full-fledged news story or feature.

This could be a mixed blessing. It can dramatically increase the exposure of your news item, but it also means you lose control over the copy. You have to put trust and faith in the newspaper—and specifically in a reporter—to accurately report what you want to say.

A plant manager for an auto parts manufacturer was understandably proud of his employees on the night shift. Their quick response in applying a tourniquet and calling 911 had been credited with saving a fellow employee's life after a freak industrial accident. After those employees were cited by the governor for their efforts, the manager called the local newspaper to report the story. He began to have second thoughts about that call when the reporter who showed up seemed to focus more on the details of the accident then the heroism angle. When his request to read the finished story before it went to press was denied, he became even more concerned. His worries were expressed to the newspaper's editor about the direction the reporter seemed to be taking with the story, and he was assured that a fair, balanced piece would be published. The plant manager had learned, however, the difference between controlling the information sent out in a news release and trusting a reporter to produce a news story with that information.

In dealing with the media, the first thing to keep in mind is that reporters and other newsmen and newswomen are human. Behind the big printing presses and barrels of black ink and hunched over the computer keyboards are real people. While the character of reporters as individuals varies immensely, a little arrogance seems to go along with the position. That's understandable because it takes a certain type of personality and attitude to hold a job that requires someone to constantly stick his nose into other people's business. And a thick skin must be developed to endure having your work critiqued by thousands of readers at least once a week and possibly every day. Add to that a degree of skepticism. It has been said that the credo of the hard-nosed journalist is "If your mother says she loves you, check it out."

But getting a news release turned into a news story doesn't have to be like having a rabid Mike Wallace pounding on your door with a *60 Minutes* camera crew in tow. In most cases, you have invited this attention with your press release or story request, and there are ways you can maintain control. Here's how to do that:

- **Set the agenda.** Just as the angle can set the tone for the press release, it can do the same for the news story. When being interviewed by the reporter, present the information based on the angle you have chosen and keep referring back to it. Writers are always searching for a good lead for their stories, and the ready-made one you suggest just might strike the reporter's fancy.

• **Provide source material.** Supply background information in writing when applicable. Nobody minds having his or her job made a little easier. A release highlighting the most important points of your story can be handed over during the interview just in case these points don't make it into the reporter's notes. Written materials also help ensure that any of your quotes lifted from those pages will be accurate.

• **Guide without manipulation.** There might be a downside or aspect of your story that will look or sound bad in print. You should be prepared to steer the interview away from that item or, when unavoidable, to address it quickly and then move on to a part of the story that you feel may be of more interest to the reporter and readers. Whatever you do, don't whine, "Do we have to put that in the story?" Even if you get the reporter to completely ignore a well-known problem, chances are that an editor will notice this omission and have the reporter call back with follow-up questions. News people's instincts are often aroused by details they feel are being withheld from them and attempts to conceal that information can actually direct more attention to it. By facing up to the unflattering item right away and dealing with it in a nonchalant way, it may just seem less newsworthy to the interviewer.

• **Be truthful.** Being less than honest on a matter that will find its way into print is a big mistake. Someone, somewhere will probably know, and it can be both embarrassing and dangerous to be caught in a lie. It can hurt not only your credibility but also the reputation of any organization or business you represent. Many reporters take pleasure in finding and pointing out contradictions in what people say, which can follow you in future news stories.

A young banker in Charlotte, N.C. who seemed to be on the fast track in the business of high finance, noted in his bio that he had won a medal in the Olympic Games. That "fact" was regularly repeated in newspaper profiles about him and often mentioned when he was introduced for speaking engagements. Such claims, however, easily can be checked. Eventually, someone who actually had competed in the Olympics called the newspaper to question the banker's purported accomplishments. It was revealed that he had never qualified for the Olympics, let alone won a medal. That discovery led to other investigations that revealed further discrepancies on his resume, and brought his promising banking career to an end.

You don't have to be a prominent banker, or a well-known newspaper columnist, or even the President of the United States, to be undone by an untruth. Anyone who is being interviewed needs to be especially careful not to play games with the truth.

- **Don't stonewall.** Often subjects in the news will refuse to provide information even in cases where that information is considered public record. In many instances this only makes reporters get their backs up and become more tenacious about seeking the information. It also harms any cooperative relationship that you would like to develop with the newspaper to help bring your message to the public.

Television commentator and newspaper columnist Andy Rooney believes that news reporting is made more difficult than it needs to be because, "… half the world is trying to hide the truth from the other half." There is usually so much information available that often the best thing to do is to provide too much rather than not enough. A reporter who is sent on an assignment will not go away empty-handed. An unknown hard-boiled editor is credited with the timeless line, "There are two kinds of reporters: ones that bring back the story and ones that bring back excuses." A man who was involved with a land development dispute with a city in Central Florida had repeatedly evaded giving comments on the controversy. The newspaper already had the city's information, but wanted his side as well. He finally called the paper—after the story had run—to complain about what was published. When the editor told him of the numerous times the paper had tried to get in touch with him he admitted that he had deliberately avoided the reporter's calls, thinking that then the paper wouldn't publish the story. The story did run, but it didn't included his side or present the issues the way he wanted them portrayed.

That story involved a small town, but even the U.S. Air Force and a large multinational company like Nike aren't immune from falling into that trap. It happened to the Air Force in an incident involving pilot 1st, Lt. Kelly Flinn who was accused of having an affair with a married officer, but was able to avoid a court martial by arguing her case before the public through a media blitz. *The American Journalism Review*, among others, pointed out that Flinn's public relations efforts focused much of the media debate on the charge of adultery and the supposedly selective prosecution of a female officer. The Air Force, on the other hand, was slow to press its case and emphasize the more serious charges of disobeying orders and lying in a sworn statement.

Nike officials were seemingly reluctant to respond quickly to allegations that its Asian factory workers were being exploited, according to the *Wall Street Journal*. It was a while before the athletic shoe manufacturer countered with information that put the pay and working conditions in the context of the culture with which it was dealing overseas.

In both cases, however, the public relations damage had been done. The Air Force ended up giving Lt. Flinn a general discharge, and the Nike flap resulted in the canceling of some contracts with foreign manufacturers.

On this point, former U.S. Senator Alan Simpson said it best: "When (reporters are) after your ass, answer the phone."

• **Provide direct answers.** A good rule of thumb is to respond to a straightforward question with a straightforward, honest answer. That way you're much less likely to leave anything open to interpretation.

• **Avoid saying "no comment."** A "no comment" response to a reporter's question is better than avoiding the reporter's calls completely, but not much better. While you always have a right to decline an interview request, doing so may imply to the reporter—and eventually to the reader or other ultimate consumer—that you have something to hide. It is better to offer some general statement or explain why you cannot make a comment.

• **Don't talk too much.** A technique used by some reporters, especially during telephone interviews, is to insert long silences after a response. Interview subjects are often uncomfortable with the silent treatment and try to fill the void by continuing to speak, ending up saying more than they intended to say. The solution is to just fight silence with silence until the reporter gives up and goes on to another question.

• **Appeal to a reporter's discretion.** Like a cop on the beat, a reporter has some discretion about how he performs his job—in this case what to report and not to report. If there is a question that makes you uncomfortable or that you think can hurt your cause, explain what the problem could be.

Make sure that it is clear up front that what you say is "off the record." Too often, someone will chatter on with all kinds of tantalizing observations and revealing quotes while a reporter is feverishly jotting down notes, only to say afterward, "You're not going to use any of that, are you?" The answer may vary. Some reporters will argue that a request to go off the record that is not made beforehand can't be considered valid. Even those who will honor the interview subject's after-the-fact request still will have recorded some things that may prove too tempting to the reporter or an editor to keep out of print.

• **Use repetition.** Assertiveness trainers advise their students to repeat an important point or request three times to make sure it is clearly communicated. The same technique can be used to emphasize points in interviews. It may be annoying, but those points sure won't be easily missed or forgotten.

• **Don't demand prior review.** Many people who grant an interview ask for something that seems like a simple courtesy but is, in fact, taboo in newspaperdom: the right to read the story before it is printed. If a subject demands such a condition many reporters and editors mention the words "prior restraint," which equates in many journalists' minds to censorship.

The prohibition about letting a subject read a story before publication comes from a concern that objectivity will be lost if the newspaper cedes control to the subject. A person who is part of the story could demand that an unflattering observation be removed from the piece, or may otherwise try to alter the angle.

So how does an interview subject ensure accuracy?

Many reporters and editors will permit quotes or other parts of a completed piece to be read to a story source or subject prior to publication. Better yet, during an interview, and after an important point is made, a subject should ask a reporter to repeat what was said to make sure there is a clear understanding of the information being imparted. But watch out when a reporter says something like, "in other words," and then proceeds to interpret what you have said. Unless those "other words" convey exactly what you meant in a more understandable form, you should insist that only your original statement be put on the record.

• **Request pre-interview review.** Ask to review anticipated questions before the interview. This may not always be possible or permissible, but it can't hurt to ask and it is an immense help in preparing for an interview. It is still wise, however, to anticipate other questions and decide how you might respond to them. It is also advisable to ask the reporter what angle or approach he intends to take.

• **Be prepared.** Make a checklist of important points you want to make and refer to it, checking off each point. If caught off guard by reporters on the phone, Dr. Sharon Smith Pennell, associate professor of journalism at Appalachian State University and an elected county school board member, recommends asking them to call back in a few minutes. This provides time to get your thoughts together. Keep in mind, however, that the return call should be made to accommodate the reporter's deadline if you want to be sure to get your comments into the story. To prepare for a tough interview do what trial lawyers do in preparing their witnesses for testimony. Have someone coach you on the hardest questions that may be asked and practice your responses. Ask in advance of the interview whether any photos will be taken so that you can literally put your best face forward.

• **Talk face-to-face.** Arrange for the interview to be conducted in person rather than over the telephone. Communicating face-to-face helps humanize both the subject and reporter and often makes discussions more comfortable. Encourage reporters to call back if they have any further questions because some may then feel more comfortable confirming information from their notes if they know additional inquires are welcome. Also make sure you get the reporter's name, phone number and extension (or e-mail address) in case you think of something later that should have been included.

• **Don't get too comfortable.** Be aware that reporters will often save their toughest questions for the end of the interview. They know that bringing up a controversial topic can abruptly end an interview and send them back to the paper empty-handed so they want to make sure they have answers to the easy questions first. If such issues exist, don't be surprised if they don't lead off the questioning and be prepared for when they do eventually come up.

• **Think in terms of the reader.** A reporter I knew used a technique that often proved helpful. He ended every interview with the same question, "Is there anything I've forgotten to ask you that you think our readers should know?" Don't be shy about volunteering information you believe is relevant even if you haven't been asked. Remember that your audience is not the interviewer, but the hundreds or thousands of readers who will eventually see the story.

• **Avoid jargon.** Avoid technical language. It is better that you explain to readers in simple words what you are talking about than have a reporter or editor attempt to interpret what you said.

Making contact

Most story tips or ideas will go through an editor who should be contacted by phone or by way of a short query letter. The letter should explain any background required to understand the subject and suggest the story angle. Remember to stress the local connection and the reason such a story would be of interest to the newspaper's readers. More information on how to engage an editor's interest is provided in Chapter 16, which explains how quickly a piece of correspondence can go from the in-basket to the wastebasket.

Many editors and reporters have e-mail addresses but still prefer receiving correspondence by mail or telephone. Those who are comfortable communicating over the Internet will often have their e-mail addresses prominently displayed in the paper. If a reporter or columnist has an e-mail address listed at the bottom of his or her story or column, that's an open invitation for readers to contact the writer that way. Online pitches should be kept short, no longer than ten lines. The writer should include an e-mail address along with a daytime and evening telephone number.

Don't send invitation cards as a substitute for a letter, phone call or e-mail coverage request. Editors and other newspaper staff members receive many invitations to banquets, parties and open houses. They can't be expected to discern between those that are intended as social invitations of a personal nature and those that are meant as coverage requests that are strictly business. Also, don't expect editors to be able to assign photographers and reporters to dinner meetings or awards presentations. While the organizations involved may believe that a free meal is a tempting incentive to the working press, reporters' and photographers' time is being charged to the paper and in such cases they often end up getting paid more for eating and socializing than for reporting and taking pictures.

10. Oops!

*One has the right to be wrong in a
democracy.*

Claude Pepper
Congressman
1946

To err is human.

To err on a daily basis is journalism.

At least sometimes it seems that way when you're dealing with tens of thousands of words in a variety of articles bound to touch somebody in some way. Too often it's the wrong way. But as inspirational speaker and author Jim Davidson notes, "The fact is, the only people who don't make mistakes are in the cemetery."

In his book, *A Good Life*, former Washington Post editor Ben Bradlee explains, "We journalists have thin skins because we are so often criticized. Often enough, we have it coming, because we make mistakes. Lots of them, and our mistakes hang out there for the world to see for at least twenty-four hours and frequently longer."

Journalists, however, do want to get it right—preferably the first time. If not, then in a subsequent correction. Each newspaper has its own policies on corrections. In some cases the corrected information will appear on the same page, and even in the same spot, as the original error.

So if the mistake occurred on the front page, the correction will appear there as well. In other cases, however, the correction will be printed on a subsequent page. This seems to validate the common complaint that the erroneous information is played up while the "true facts" are buried inside the paper where few who read the original flawed report might see them. That's one thing the readers of newspapers like *The Mobile (Ala.) Register* can't complain about. Since 1978, *The Register* has had a policy of running all corrections on the front page. *The Chicago Tribune* is even making sure corrections are included on the archived stories posted online. Notices of the correction are placed on the top of the story on the Web site and at the place in the story where the error was made. Several newspapers and online news sites have Web pages set up specifically for correcting previously reported information.

Despite a newspaper's best efforts, errors occur for a variety of reasons. Sometimes they stem from misinformation provided by the source. This is one reason many papers insist on written news releases rather than accepting information phoned in. When a written news release is submitted, an error can more easily be traced to its source and accountability assigned for any lack of accuracy. Some papers, such as the *Chicago Tribune*, have a system for tracking errors and explaining how they happened, according to the *American Journalism Review*. For example, when one *Tribune* news staffer was asked how an error occurred, the reporter candidly wrote, "I do not mean to make excuses and am not trying to be funny, but insomnia caused me to get a mere four hours sleep the night before and my left eye felt like a hot needle was sticking in it. I was really fading when I wrote this story."

In many cases, mistakes can be avoided if a news clerk, reporter or editor would only make an additional phone call, or two or three…to verify information. What often keeps those extra calls from being made is that ever-present deadline. If everything written in the newspaper was double- or triple-checked through additional contacts, very little would be available for publication for each day's or week's edition, particularly at small papers with limited staffs. The corrections policy at the *San Jose (Calif.) Mercury News* explains it this way, "The business of journalism asks humans to do something unnatural: to synthesize complex material on deadline. Occasionally all of us will err while performing that task."

Sometimes it is just a matter of a clean miss by an editor who may have too much confidence in a reporter and too little time to verify that reporter's work. One case that comes to mind involved a photo caption of a group of people volunteering in a soup kitchen. Two of the young men were identified as Jehovah's Witness missionaries with the titles of "elder." A woman who called the paper the next day noted that the elders were actually Mormon missionaries affiliated with the Church of Christ of Latter Day Saints. The reporter may not have seen much difference between the two religious affiliations, but many others, especially those who belong to those churches, certainly do.

Computer spelling programs and grammar checkers help editors spot and eliminate many errors, but even this technology can be responsible for inaccuracies. Consider this correction printed by the *Mountain Xpress* in Asheville, North Carolina: "We regret that Sonja Controis' name was inadvertently changed to "Song Connotes" during our spell-check process..."

Most errors simply involve names, dates or numbers that were incorrectly published. These are usually easy to rectify. The real damage done by errors is to reputations, as in cases where people or businesses are named in connection with crimes or compromising situations with which they were not involved. Such information often comes from local police reports or court records. In such cases reporters are advised to rely on that documentation and include ages and addresses to reduce the possibility of mistaken identity. This doesn't guarantee that an innocent person will never be implicated in wrongdoing, because police officers make mistakes too, but it does provide a firm foundation for a news report. When reporters use unidentified sources as the basis for directing suspicion without collaborating documentation, it is a lot more difficult to justify publication.

Clarifications

When the information printed was correct but may have created a mistaken impression in the minds of some readers, an editor may allow a clarification to be printed. *The Wall Street Journal*, for example, publishes a box titled "Clarifications and Amplifications" on page 2A almost daily to clear up questions about previously published stories. That spot included the following item:

> "**THE DETROIT FREE PRESS** says it never believed that an April Fools' Day news release about the **Public Broadcasting Service** buying **Time Warner Inc.** was true, as suggested in an article yesterday. The Free Press said that it knows a spoof when it sees one, and that it contacted the Associated Press simply to learn more about the origin of the release."

One situation where a clarification was used effectively in a newspaper involved a police report that noted the address of a home from which an ambulance was called to pick up a stabbing victim following a drug deal. A family member from that home later called asking that it be made clear the residents of that address had no connection to the drug deal, but had only called for the ambulance after the wounded man stumbled into their yard from the intersection where the crime had actually occurred. The facts in the original report were correct, but the impression they made was misleading. Therefore a clarification was appropriate.

Updates

There are instances where the initial report is correct, but the situation changes over time. In such cases an update may be more appropriate than a correction or clarification.

Such a situation may involve a person who was charged with a crime but was later cleared when those charges were dropped or dismissed by a court. Even if newspapers include the original arrest in a report from the log at the police station or jail, they may not pick up on the disposition of the case at the courthouse. If a person is cleared of a crime and wants to set the record straight he should request an update. As noted before, newsrooms can only follow a few cases all the way through the legal system, and these are usually the more serious ones in which readers show a great interest. Newspapers, however, will update any previously reported case when its disposition is brought to their attention.

Updates can also be used to follow-up on other news reports covering everything from the health of a young cancer victim to a restaurant's poor health inspection rating. An update request should appeal to an editor's sense of fairness and interest in keeping the public informed about the latest developments in news that affects the community.

Setting it right

Some papers have their own set policies and procedures regarding mistakes of fact, but the best way to request a correction is to call the reporter and explain the discrepancy. If you aren't satisfied with the response from the writer, or the error occurred in a news release, contact the editor. A few papers also have a reader advocate or ombudsman, an independent monitor of fairness and accuracy, who handles such complaints. (*The Virginia Pilot* calls that position a "public editor.") If all else fails, contact the publisher, whose name should appear on page 2 or on the editorial page. Have a copy of the article in question when you call or with you when you visit the office. Too often newspaper editors and publishers get calls from people who "heard" about an article that someone said was in the paper a week or so ago. A resolution is much easier when the exact wording and date of the problem piece is known.

Demanding a "retraction" can be counterproductive. Once a statement is printed it can never actually be taken back. CNN's *Newsstand* program and *Time* magazine retracted a story that alleged the U.S. used nerve gas in Laos during the Vietnam conflict, but that retraction didn't make everyone instantly forget the controversy.

Unless a mistake changes the entire meaning of the piece or makes it unreadable, it is pointless to insist that an entire article be republished in a newspaper. What a correction will do is identify where the previous error occurred, supply the correct information and in many cases explain why the mistake happened. Even when a mistake is caused by someone other than a newspaper employee, editors may still run a correction because they want to make sure information in the paper is presented as accurately as possible. This can sometimes involve writing an entire editorial or column about the mistake, if a two- or three-line correction is not sufficient.

Several years ago I wrote a column after being called to task at a county board meeting for a story I had written about the board's voting record. A board member complained that the vote totals were taken out of context, without the benefit of someone at the paper having attended the meetings to see how the decisions were made. He said he didn't appreciate what the article was suggesting—that the board was just a rubber stamp for whatever exceptions were requested to the zoning code. The follow-up column I wrote conceded that the board member was right. Even though the original article didn't contain any "errors of fact," it could have been misleading from the perspective taken on the story.

"We get enough people mad at us by maintaining objectivity and doing our job, without making the mistake of being biased," the column read. "I'm realistic enough to know that remaining totally objective in every situation is humanly impossible, but it is a goal we should strive to be aware of at all times. I'll try to keep that in mind." Few articles I had ever written received the attention and as many compliments as that apology piece.

The *Milwaukee Journal Sentinel* felt compelled to run an entire story to correct a previously published front-page account involving school spending. Data on the local school system's spending per student was used as a basis for the original story, but the figure reported turned out to be incorrect by a significant amount, which changed the entire thrust of the piece. The lead of the first story said, "South Milwaukee, you're No. 1." The newspaper's front-page story the next day started out with "South Milwaukee, you're not No. 1."

Besides the issue of fairness, it is to the newspaper's benefit economically to listen to aggrieved readers and respond to requests for corrections. Press attorneys say that admitting mistakes and doing something to set the record straight can help avoid libel lawsuits. Even if a correction doesn't stop a legal claim, it can make the newspaper's defense stronger before a judge or jury.

In seeking a correction, however, reminding a newspaper editor of his obligation is often more effective than threatening legal action. Among the recommendations for newspaper corrections policies endorsed by United States members of the Organization of News Ombudsmen are:

• Be aggressive in admitting mistakes and setting the record straight. When you learn of an error of substance, publish a correction.

• Make it easy for readers to point out potential errors in the newspaper.

• Make sure necessary corrections run in a timely fashion.

• Anchor corrections. Make it easy for readers to find them.

• Make sure news, feature, sports, entertainment and editorial operations apply similar standards of accuracy and follow the same corrections procedures.

Maintaining credibility is often just as important to publishers and editors as avoiding legal exposure. It is a concern that has grown in recent years as more and more news content has been added to the Internet. A 1999 survey by the Pew Research Center For The People & The Press reported that two-thirds of the public believes the press tries to cover up its mistakes—a jump since 1985, when just over half of the public said so.

"Corrections are important for credibility," says Frank Sennett, editor of newcitynet.com, an alternative-press portal. He calls the desire to cover up mistakes the "dark side" of news sites. Sennett, whose efforts to get news services to admit their mistakes and apologize for them led to the creation of his Web site Slipup.com, sees a vital need for online news standards for corrections because more people are getting their news from the Web.

In an apology to readers over the publication of *Newsstand's* nerve gas story, Time Managing Editor Walter Isaacson summed up the feelings shared by many news publications. "Our credibility is our most important asset. When we make mistakes, it's important to be open and honest about them, get all the facts out as quickly as possible and try to set the record straight. And to say we're sorry. We are."

Choose your battles

As a county school board member, ASU journalism professor Dr. Sharon Pennell has maintained a good working relationship with the press. It helps that she doesn't quibble about every possible misquote or error if the mistake doesn't substantially alter the meaning of her message. So when she does file a rare complaint, the reporter and editor know it's a serious concern. "Choose your battles and what you're willing to bleed over," she advises.

But it is also important to ask for corrections when inaccuracies are spotted, and not just as a way to show those know-it-alls down at the paper that they messed up. In this digital age, a newspaper's database is forever so there is a chance that a portion of a story will be used again in a follow-up article. If a correction request isn't made, the assumption will be that everything printed before was accurate, increasing the potential for repetition of the same mistake in future newspaper articles and online reports.

When a woman called the paper to say it had spelled her name wrong in the last three stories published about her organization, she was asked why she hadn't called it to the editor's attention the first time.

"I just let it go, because I didn't think it mattered," she replied.

It did matter, to the editor, and eventually to her as well.

All's well that ends well

While newspapers never want to miss an error prior to publication, there are rare occasions when misprints don't turn out to be such a bad thing.

A home furnishings store many years ago ran an advertisement in a newspaper to promote a sale on bedding and mattresses with a headline that was supposed to read "Better Bedding Week." Instead, the ad carried the headline "Better Breeding Week." The humorous misprint received a lot of attention and helped the store sell plenty of mattresses, resulting in one of the merchant's most successful advertising campaigns.

Would that most mistakes turned out as well. Most editors, however, would agree with the Post's Bradlee who said, "Corrections are more fun to read than make."

11. Strictly Business

> *Business people assume that if we*
> *(the press) are not advocates, we are*
> *therefore adversaries. We ask the*
> *tough questions not because we are*
> *opponents, but because the questions*
> *need to be asked.*
>
> *John T. Harding*
> *News executive*
> *1994*

Businesses, even in smaller markets, spend thousands of dollars on advertisements and promotions, so it is surprising that a great many pass up the opportunity for *free* publicity in their local newspaper.

I'm not talking about the mythical "free ad" here. Many promotions are also news. Much of what area businesses do is of interest not only to their employees and stockholders, but also to the people within their markets, and therefore is legitimate news worthy of free publicity.

Most papers have a page or section specifically set aside for this kind of news. And some items that can significantly impact the local economy or that involve unusual promotions or operations can be considered for feature articles and even front-page placement.

Owners of The Gourmet Garage in New York City knew their one thousand dollar annual advertising budget wouldn't go far in promoting a new restaurant. Creative use of publicity and promotions, however, attracted the free media publicity which made their venture an almost over-night success. They did it by hiring a publicist, but many business owners don't even have to go to that expense.

The following are some examples of business news items that are usually solicited and printed in the paper:

• **Hiring and employee promotions.** People are always interested in what their neighbors are up to, so such listings draw good readership. For the businesses, it allows them to crow about adding a well-known local salesman they have lured away from a competitor, or to give an additional pat on the back to an employee who has won an award or earned a promotion.

Other savvy business people use such public listings to their advantage in another way. Anyone from an insurance salesman to a politician can make a good impression with a current or prospective customer by sending a clipping and a congratulations note to someone whose accomplishment has been mentioned in the paper.

• **Employee of the month/year.** Because of the sheer number of internal organizational honors that newspapers have the potential to receive, publication policies vary from paper to paper. Business pages in small markets or that need the copy may take them until the volume becomes too unmanageable. Other papers take all they can get. When in doubt, call the business editor (off deadline of course) and ask. Benefits of this category are similar to those stated in the preceding item.

• **Expansions.** Releases can be about both physical plant expansions (which can also make for some good photo opportunities), and additional services. Keeping the paper informed of such changes gives a business the opportunity to get continuing coverage after the big splash of a grand opening. When a convenience store in one small town added a full-service deli, the owner sent a news release about it. It arrived at a time when the business editor needed a local picture for his page. He ended up sending a photographer and the storeowner got more coverage than he expected. Few businesses can survive today without continuous improvement, so why not let everybody in town know what you're doing to stay competitive?

• **New business.** This might be the most newsworthy category of all for several reasons. First, consumers are always interested in any new restaurant, store or service planning to come into the community. Other businesses are also interested in what type of new competition they may be facing. Second, workers are interested in the job opportunities this may bring. And third, local government officials have an interest in how additional business may stimulate the area economy and impact the tax base.

• **Awards and honors.** These can be for the business itself and/or an individual employee. Either way, the publicizing of an industry, trade or customer service award certainly can't hurt a business' efforts to establish a quality brand name. Having that honor noted in a news item can often enhance that announcement as opposed to only trumpeting it in an ad. When a car dealer in one market won a national award for customer service, it was news at the local paper from both an editorial and advertising standpoint. Outside awards presented by a state or national organization independent of the specific company are usually deemed more newsworthy than an honor that comes from the business or corporation itself. For example, a regional GM award for a local Chevrolet dealership is not as impressive as recognition from the U.S. Automobile Association for that same business.

• **Training or certifications.** Publicizing the fact that an employee has attended a seminar, successfully completed a training course or attained a professional or technical certification is another form of promotion. Such announcements not only speak to the competence of the workers, but also to the commitment of the business itself in improving the quality of its service.

• **Public speaking**. When a representative of a local business gives a talk about the state of his or her industry to any group or organization it may be news. A CEO from the headquarters of a company that has a local branch in the area and who speaks locally also makes for good news copy, whether that speech is covered by a newspaper reporter or described in a news release submitted to the paper. For example, a local electric cooperative chief executive officer's comments on the deregulation of the electric utility industry and its possible impact on customers has the potential to attract the attention of several news outlets.

• **People features.** There's no reason that business stories can't be people stories as well. Every employee of a local company no doubt has interesting hobbies or experiences that would make good feature articles. An employee of a telephone company who collected old glass insulators that were once standard equipment on telephone poles was turned into a good feature. The phone company's public relations representative made it easy on the newspaper staff by sending in the story and a photo, both of which received good play.

• **Business anniversaries**. Most new businesses don't make it through the first year, according to economic development officials, so a commercial venture that continues to serve its community for 10, 20 or 50 years is news. A business reaching such a milestone should not only promote it with paid advertisements but with news releases as well. With staff turnover being frequent at many companies, this also goes for the exceptional employees who have worked at a business for long periods. And remember that people aren't the only ones who celebrate anniversaries. Duke Power Corp. recently issued a press release about an unusual milestone—the 75th anniversary of a hydroelectric station that is still helping to provide power to its area customers.

• **Landmarks.** You may have relocated your businesses 10 years ago, but there still may be a story opportunity connected to your previous location. Maybe your former building was the oldest in downtown or the first multi-story structure in the city or county. One business owner notified the local newspaper that his former service station, which was in the process of being torn down to accommodate a new drug store, was the last of the original buildings on what was once the town's traffic circle. Several people were more than willing to reminisce about the old days for a feature story, and the owners also had an opportunity to mention something about their present location and services as they reminisced about what was offered in the "old days."

• **Surveys.** Information about consumer trends not only makes interesting stories but also provides good opportunities for charts and graphics to accompany a story. When the local cable TV franchise in one county surveyed its customers to see what new channels they wanted to see, the local newspaper gave the story front-page play. Readers are especially interested in seeing how something they had a part in turned out and how their choices compare to others.

Tabulations from such a survey provide source material for simple charts that can be created with computer software commonly used by companies and newspapers. Business page editors seek graphics to help break up the type, so if the information you want to provide can be turned into graphs or charts, it may have a better chance of catching their attention. For example, a news release from a national floral association at first seemed to an editor to be a pure promotional gimmick. But just when it looked as though the only thing that was going to survive the garbage can was the big, shiny paper clip holding the pages together he spotted the graphics that accompanied the piece. The association had converted information from the release about the gifts most appreciated on Secretaries Day, and seeing it in that form made the information much more appealing and usable.

• **Corporate releases.** News from the out-of-town corporate headquarters of a local business may be of minimal interest to the readers of the local *Town Crier News*, but not necessarily. A local rewrite to point out the significance to area folks can make it more enticing to the newspaper.

One example of this was a release mailed to a paper by the Ford Motor Company about the statewide effort of Ford dealers to provide hurricane relief in North Carolina. It would have been more newsworthy if the local Ford dealership issued a release describing its role in the effort or pointing out how area residents or programs were involved.

• **Seminars.** Many businesses offer informational meetings that are open to the public. Health care companies such as hospitals may put on regular seminars on health-related issues, and investment firms may offer forums on certain financial topics. While these businesses are certainly welcome to publicize their events through paid advertising, there is often enough public interest involved to have them qualify as news items too.

Release forms

Providing business information to the newspaper can be easier than writing a release from scratch. Papers usually have forms available with blank spaces to be filled in by business personnel. If the paper doesn't have its own business form, use the basic news release format or the sample release form in Appendix C of this book.

Even if local businesses don't have anything to report or publicize right now, it is a good idea to file away a blank release form for use as a master. Make copies as news items develop and send them in. Along with the form, don't forget to send photos, especially when an employee promotion or award is involved. A mug shot (a head-and-shoulders photo) is usually appropriate for such submissions.

Remember, however, that a business release is a news item and will be treated that way by the editor. This means that, unlike an ad, it may not be published exactly as it was submitted. Some parts may be rearranged to fit the newspaper's style and some information eliminated to accommodate space restrictions or because of the individual paper's policies on the type of information published on the business page.

Whether or not a business form is used or a release is written from scratch, a commercial enterprise should develop and use a standard ending paragraph that describes its mission and impact on the business community. While editors are most likely to cut releases from the bottom where the least important information resides, there are times when an additional inch or two of copy is needed to fill a hole. An example of a closing paragraph is this one used by Broyhill Furniture Industries on every release it issues:

> Broyhill Furniture Industries is one of the largest full-line furniture manufacturers in the world with more than 7,200 employees. Broyhill is the most recognized line

> of furniture among consumers and
> provides products for living rooms,
> dining rooms, bedrooms, home
> offices and home entertainment.
> Broyhill Furniture is headquartered
> in Lenoir, North Carolina and is
> part of Furniture Brands
> International (NYSE:FBN), also the
> parent company of Lane and
> Thomasville.

The fact that a company with "the most recognized line of furniture" finds it necessary to remind readers of that fact every time it issues a news release is a good indication of the value of including such branding information in a stock paragraph.

Business vs. the media

Mistrust of the media in general unfortunately inhibits some companies from submitting news items.

Part of that comes from the unnatural dual personality of a newspaper. After all, how many other companies can have one department (Advertising) soliciting business from a customer while another department (News) is working to report on some unflattering aspect involving that same customer? Such a situation makes for a tough sell, and many an advertising account (and advertising salesperson's commission) has been lost because of routine news reporting.

It is also not uncommon for a big advertiser in the newspaper to believe his advertising space purchases grant him some special privileges when it comes to news coverage. Not only does he expect a reporter and photographer to be available whenever he gives out a donation or gets a new product line, but he believes he can prevent negative news about his business from appearing in the paper. The ethical code at most newspapers would prove him wrong. Ideally, a business relationship between and advertiser and the newspaper should not affect news coverage either way. Most publishers, while concerned about ad revenue also understand the role of the newsroom, and usually insist only that everyone be treated fairly.

Philosophically, news people and business owners tend to be on opposite sides of the political spectrum. Traditionally, big business has been viewed as the enemy by a liberal press that has cast itself in the role of protector of the little guy, the environment and the wronged. While that advocacy role is still a vital one for newspapers, there has also been a major reality check in recent years as news people have been forced to recognize that they are in business too. This point has hit home with editors who attend financial meetings with publishers and who feel the impact of decreasing ad sales revenue and circulation numbers. When editorial staffing is cut back and the news features budget is decimated, it tends to get an editor's attention.

This doesn't mean that big business gets a free ride and that news people have joined what many still think of as "the dark side." It does mean, however, that the solid wall that existed between the editorial and business sides of many newspapers has become more porous in recent years. Editors may be a little more sensitive to the needs and difficulties of businesses, but not to the point of overlooking newsworthy stories about health and safety violations, major layoffs or lawsuits involving commercial concerns. In many newsrooms an understanding has developed toward better serving the needs of business from the standpoint of the economic well-being of the community.

The move toward a closer relationship between business and news at the *Los Angeles Times* attracted a lot of attention in the newspaper industry. Having business managers working with editors on planning was considered a radical change for one of the largest newspapers in the country, but is not so foreign to the editor of a small weekly whose job has always involved crossing departmental lines.

Damage control

When disaster does strike, businesses can often do themselves a favor by using damage control rather than trying to hide problems. If they think they can keep a major layoff or regulatory problem secret for long they are mistaken. Every company has employees who are more than happy to phone in an anonymous tip to the newspaper, and people who have just lost their jobs may figure they don't have much else to lose.

A county hospital had spent a lot of money in recent years building up its image as the area's best health care provider. But when a state regulatory board cited its pharmacy for irregularities in handling prescription drugs, the hospital's public relations efforts ground to a halt. Yet this was when astute public relations and a well-worded press statement could have made a big difference.

Rather than assuming a defensive posture and waiting for reporters to call for comment, the hospital should have issued a news release pointing out from the beginning the fact that the previous procedural violations cited by the board had been addressed and did not affect the delivery of local health care services.

Similarly, a company experiencing a layoff can explain what it is doing to retrain employees and help them find other employment, the reasons for the reduction in workforce and how it will help to make the local firm more financially viable. Experts in crisis management say organizations have the first 24 hours to control or shape the story. They should think in terms of headlines, because those printed sound bites are what will form the initial perception in the reading public's mind. Whatever information comes out later will be influenced by the perceptions developed from those original reports.

Being prepared to put a positive angle, or spin, on bad news can mean the difference between being perceived by the reading public as going *bankrupt* or being seen as undergoing a *reorganization.*

It is crucial to have a crisis plan in place that details how worst case scenarios will be managed and who will manage them. Everyone in the organization should be aware of the existence of that plan so that a united front and response is presented. A crisis plan should not be put on the shelf and forgotten after it is created. To be effective it must be reviewed and updated at regular intervals—every six months or at least once a year. Many public relations firms offer help in developing corporate crisis plans or reviewing existing policies.

Trying to conceal information also arouses the curiosity of reporters who thrive on the idea of uncovering news. If a company comes forward with the information right off the bat and presents it to the newspaper, it can take a little of the wind out of a crusading reporter's sails.

It is a good idea not to wait until disaster strikes before introducing yourself to the local press. Identify the reporters or editors at the newspapers who will be handling stories concerning your business and make sure they have the name, telephone number, pager number and/or e-mail address of a contact person. It doesn't matter if that person is located at a local business office, an out-of-town corporate headquarters or a trade association. The most important thing is that he or she be accessible to answer questions.

If a story does break, make sure your side is represented. Good reporters will want to give you that opportunity anyway, but they may not be able to get to the right people at the right time without some advance planning on your part. Often some knowledgeable comments can mitigate a public relations problem or at least put it in a more favorable context for the readers.

Above all, be honest when facing a crisis. Being caught in one lie or distributing misinformation—whether intentionally or by accident—can taint everything else a company spokesperson has to say in the reader's mind. Rather than speculate about information that is not available to satisfy the media's questions just say, "I don't know." Then find out. Appearing temporarily ignorant is much better than appearing permanently dishonest.

12. SELLING A STORY

The First Amendment guarantees freedom of speech, but not funding of freedom of speech.

Herb Shayne
Businessman
1994

Jonathan Jay believed he had a story idea that no newspaper could resist. It was about a new sport he had invented—kind of a cross between football and baseball, but that he guaranteed was bound to be bigger than both some day. And it was the local editor's lucky day, because he was going to give the newspaper an exclusive by selling the right to tell the world all about his creation.

But this was not Jonathan's lucky day.

The editor explained to him that while someone from the sports department might be available to talk to him about his new game, it was not the paper's policy to pay for news stories. It's not the policy of most newspapers to do so either.

Jonathan couldn't understand that. He was only asking for $500 for the *exclusive* rights. He knew the paper he had visited was small, but he also knew that the company that owned it—*The New York Times*—

could easily afford his asking price. And part of the deal he was proposing would give *The Times* the rights to publicize his new sport as well. He urged the editor to seriously consider his offer and to call his "people" at *The Times* and gauge their interest as well. Already knowing what the response would be, the local editor called a senior editor in The New York Times Regional Newspaper Group and confirmed what he had already told Jonathan. Eventually the game inventor relented and the local paper ended up doing a sports feature story on his idea. But there was never any payment involved.

There are a lot of good reasons for bringing story ideas to the local newspaper. Making money is not one of them. Some nationally circulated papers have paid large sums for sensational headlines, but the mainstream press does not operate that way. Tight newsroom budgets don't include a line item titled "story idea payments" or "hot tip fees."

There might be some expenses incurred by reporters in getting a story, such as travel costs or copying fees for public records, but the most a source might get is a free lunch—if that meal can be justified as a legitimate business expense.

It is not that newspapers are cheap, although, like any business in recent years, cost control is emphasized. The primary reason no payments are made for "scoops" is the newspaper's need to maintain its credibility. Someone who anticipates a big payoff for a compelling story may be more likely to exaggerate or even fabricate details to make a sale. The fact that someone is willing to sell what they know to a newspaper also would put controls on information that do not sit well with reporters and editors who require unfettered access.

News tips

Believe it or not, newspapers get a lot of story ideas and tips every day from people who have no expectation of monetary reward. That doesn't mean they don't have something to gain from news coverage.

Often someone will see the need for public recognition of a selfless deed in the community, or will want to see their own accomplishments publicized. But just as often something negative is called to a newspaper's attention. Revenge, jealousy and plain nastiness can be powerful motivators, and consequently valuable news tip generators.

For example, a man called one newspaper to report on some maintenance irregularities in the school bus garage he said were jeopardizing the safety of children. It just so happens that this same person had recently been fired from his job at the garage. Although these irregularities had supposedly been going on for some time, he had only now decided to blow the whistle. A news staffer certainly has to consider the source in such cases, because he doesn't want people to use the newspaper to pursue personal vendettas. The allegations, however, were serious enough in this case for the newspaper to look into them. Reporters were able to independently confirm that state inspectors had cited the garage for certain maintenance problems. They were not as serious a threat to student safety as the source had suggested, but were certainly newsworthy.

So did the fired employee get something from the story? Probably. His former boss certainly didn't look very good in front of his bosses and the community, and the source may have gotten some satisfaction from that.

Investigating complaints

Many people assume that when they "leak" a tip to the newspaper that all the allegations—whether anonymous or attributed to the source by name—will be rushed into print in the next edition. That is not the way it works.

For instance, someone may complain (a) that he was cheated by a used car dealership, (b) is having a dispute with his landlord, (c) was sold tainted food by a supermarket, or (d) had been treated rudely by a government employee. He thinks a story about his problems should be published in the local paper. In fact, he may have even threatened the merchant, landlord, supermarket manager or government employee with retribution by the local press.

While it can be flattering to be considered the final arbiter in all local disputes, a newspaper can't fulfill that role. For one thing, smaller papers can't afford to have a full-time consumer reporter to handle complaints. And when a reporter is assigned to do such a story it too often ends up being one person's word against the other. (Yes, fairness demands that reporters have to get the other person's side of the story.) This doesn't mean that consumer complaints don't always make good news stories. If there are several people complaining or the problem can be tied to a bigger issue, such as cable TV deregulation or restaurant health inspections, the news value increases dramatically. Also, if independent confirmation or official documentation is available (such as a complaint filed in civil court, a police incident report, or a problem voiced at an open public meeting) they can provide a sound basis for a news story.

In many cases, however, a letter to the corporate office of a company or a call to the area's Better Business Bureau can be more effective than a complaint to the newspaper. Too often, people go to the newspaper as a first resort, and that's not always the most efficient or direct way to address an individual problem. The chain of command should be followed in both business and government during the initial handling of a complaint.

A newspaper newsroom provides a many-faceted service, but it can't be everything to everyone. It isn't a social service agency, a law enforcement agency, a domestic dispute mediator, a research organization, a lost and found, a vehicle of retribution, or a thank-you note or invitation provider. What can truly confuse the issue, however, is that at times and under certain circumstances, a newspaper can also be all of those things, and more.

Unnamed sources

Former U.S. Senator Alan K. Simpson, who was known for his battles with the press, referred to the use of anonymous sources as "the bane of my existence." Simpson said he had never seen an unnamed source speak well of anyone.

For various reasons, some news tips that come to the newspaper will be from anonymous sources. Sometimes they won't tell the editor or reporter who they are, and other times they'll identify themselves but ask that their names not be used in connection with any story. Unnamed sources who want to remain unidentified should let a reporter know up front that they don't want what they say attributed to them in the preparation or publication of any news story. Before they say anything, they should ask about the newspaper's policy on unidentified sources. Many newspapers will pledge unlimited confidentiality to a source. Others may be willing to keep the secret right up until a subpoena arrives requiring a reporter to appear in court and reveal the source of a story. To their credit, most newspaper staffers have been willing to go to jail to protect a source and have done so. Tim Crews, the editor and publisher of the *Sacramento Valley Mirror*, probably had more to lose than most journalists faced with the choice of giving up a source or their own freedom. He not only produced the California paper twice a week, but also delivered the 2,600 copies himself. But when Crews was ordered by a judge to reveal sources used in a story about a charge against a state highway patrol officer he refused. As a result, he spent five days in jail. Anonymous tipsters should be forewarned, however, that other journalists may not be willing to endure that much to keep your secret.

Newspaper legal counsels are usually cautious about using information from unidentified sources in a story. They argue that with the assurance of anonymity, sources may feel free to speculate, telling more than they actually know. Tom Winship, former editor of the *Boston Globe*, is more to the point: "The blind quote always is a license to lie and to exaggerate." On the rare occasions unidentified sources must be used, many editors will insist that there be at least some indication of how the source was in a position to know what is being reported. For example, the published information may be attributed to "a source close to the investigation" or "a top campaign advisor." That type of partial identification gives readers a better chance to judge the credibility of the information's source.

In some cases, the original source is not referred to at all in a story, but merely serves to point the reporter in the right direction. The source's information is then confirmed by another means and reported, as was the case with the bus garage story mentioned earlier. Reporters are always looking for documentation or official on-the-record statements to support what has been leaked because that provides a more solid basis for a story.

Paid correspondents

People who can come up with interesting story ideas and who also have the ability to write about them may be able to pry loose some money from an editor. Most newsroom budgets do contain a line item for correspondents or stringers. But aspiring part-time journalists shouldn't quit their day jobs just yet.

Many freelancers who submit stories to newspapers—especially small papers—and request payment for their efforts are often surprised at how little money is offered. Some newspapers pay a fixed amount per inch while others pay a lump sum per story, column or photo. But most don't pay enough to constitute what a reasonable person would consider a living wage. For example, the writer of a fully developed feature or travel piece with photos may be lucky to get $100 to $150 from a small daily, with no reimbursement for out-of-pocket expenses. Other stringers may have to settle for $1 to $1.50 per column inch or $6 to $8 an hour for their efforts. As a rule of thumb, the larger circulation a paper has, the more generous it can afford to be. Bigger papers and news services may be willing to offer hundreds of dollars for a single exceptional photograph. Whatever the amount paid, though, stringers aren't guaranteed regular publication of their work. In other words, it is not a steady income source.

Aside from pay, such as it is, there are other rewards that come from contributing articles to your local newspaper. For beginning writers it is often the easiest way to get published and build up a clip file of articles. At the same time it can provide some feedback to writers about their work, not only from the editors at the newspapers but also from readers. Comments may come directly to the writer or through letters to the editor.

Local columns

While some larger papers can afford to hire full-time column writers, the real money for most columnists is in syndication. The individual writer doesn't make much from each paper in which his or her column appears, but it adds up when the piece is running in hundreds of publications. For instance, an editor may pay $5 for each weekly syndicated column and three to eight times that amount to the writer of a local column. The difference is that the $15 to $40 bucks the local writer gets is 100 percent of his payment, while the $5 may be one-five hundredth of the syndicated columnist's total income from the piece. Local columnists who envision striking it rich in syndication, however, should know that competition for space on newspaper pages is fierce and syndicates are choosy about the features they agree to market.

Talk, it is said, is cheap. Writing often doesn't increase the value of those words by much.

13. YOUR TWO CENTS

*The job of the press is to encourage
debate, not to supply the public with
information.*

Christopher Lasch
Historian
1990

For evidence that people really do have a love-hate relationship with
their local newspapers, look no further than the Editorial Page.

That is where the paper's "editorial board" informs readers what it
thinks about a variety of issues. It is also where readers get to express their
thoughts on those opinions, as well as on the newspaper's stories, the condition of local roads, Aunt Edna's lemon chiffon pie and just about anything else on their minds. (All right, Edna's pie review may be stretching
most newspapers' letter eligibility standards a bit.) Sometimes readers who
make accusations of biased reporting believe they can tell newspapers
what the paper's stands are on issues before the editorial board has even
taken a stand.

Everyone has an opinion and people are often interested in what others
think as well. While a great number of readers bypass the Editorial Page
in favor of the comics or sports pages, there are many who turn to the
opinion page first—and for good reason.

Newspaper opinion pages provide an unequaled opportunity for interaction and shared insight that can help build a consensus for a community. Put simply, the editorial page is the reader's turn. Newspaper editors dictate what appears on most of the other pages of the newspaper, so on the editorial page space is provided for outside voices. Some newspaper chains have gone as far as abolishing the newspaper's own editorial views, giving over the entire page to readers. Others feel a duty to provide a subjective perspective on the news because of the unique position that news gatherers hold and their access to sources and information that may not be available to others.

No matter how much information Editorial Board members have, however, they can't always be right. The corrections that appear in newspapers every day prove that. And despite the efforts that have been made to diversify the newspaper workforce in recent years, no editorial board can know or represent the hopes, dreams, needs and status of every reader or person in the community. That is why reader opinion is so important. It helps fill in information gaps, challenge perceptions and offer solutions that may not have been considered or explored.

Editorial page editors want public opinion and encourage it. Many times readers will start a letter to the editor with "I know you won't print this but…" The fact is, newspapers do want and need opinions that differ from their stands as well as from popular beliefs. Some newspapers even state a preference for publishing letters that disagree with the newspaper's editorial positions. Editors believe that by publishing such contrary statements (even criticisms of the paper itself) they build credibility among readers. (Many large newspapers even separate their news and Editorial Page staff to draw a clear line between reporting the news and commenting on it. Because of staffing limitations, small papers are forced to cross the line by having the same people who write and edit news stories produce the editorials.)

The Editorial Page's public forum can also provide an opportunity for readers to set the record straight about published stories. Individuals who don't agree with the way facts are presented in newspaper articles or people with more information on a subject may be able to provide an addition, clarification or correction by way of a letter or guest column.

No law, not even the free speech provision in the Bill of Rights, forces newspapers to print critical opinions. Editorial page policies require it because the dissemination of ideas is one of the most important purposes of a free press.

So how do you get your two cents into the paper?

• **Letters to the editor.** This is one of the best ways to have an opinion published. The rules for letters usually appear on the editorial page of the paper. As a general guideline, letter writers are required to include their name, address and daytime and evening phone numbers (not for publication but for verification purposes). Many papers have a policy of not withholding the writer's name when publishing a letter, especially if the letter is critical of a person or organization (similar to the American justice system's policy of letting the accused know the accuser). Exceptions may be made in certain circumstances where there is good reason for anonymity, but these should be discussed with the editor. In general, newspapers will not print letters that identify the writers only as a "concerned citizen" or an "outraged mother."

The shorter the submission the better the chance of publication, especially in larger newspapers that receive hundreds of letters a week. Letters between 150 to 250 words are considered ideal, but individual newspaper preferences vary.

The *Sacramento (Calif.) Bee*, for example, publishes only about one-third of the letters it receives due to space limitations, and the average letter published is no more than 150 words. At the *Orlando (Fla.) Sentinel*, letter writers are asked to keep their submissions to 175 words or less, and at the *Honolulu Star-Bulletin* to about 200. *The Birmingham (Ala.) Post-Herald* and *Las Vegas Sun* give preference to letters of 250 words or less, and the *Tampa (Fla.) Tribune* puts its limit at 400 words. *The Key West*

(Fla.) Citizen is even more generous with its letter space, allowing up to 500 words.

Letters should stick to one point and be timely, referring to an issue or event within the last few weeks. Letters that refer to a recent story in the newspaper may get preference. To help make sure everyone gets a chance to express an opinion, many newspapers will limit the frequency of letters published from the same writers to no more than one per month.

Some letters may not be deemed suitable for publication, even short ones with a name attached, because they could be potentially libelous. These often include letters that accuse businesses or individuals of providing poor or unsafe services or being engaged in illegal activities. A newspaper could be held just as liable in publishing such "opinions" as it would be if these accusations were made in a news story without proof the statements are true. Editorial page editors also shy away from mean-spirited letters that take a cheap shot at someone, even if no legal liability is perceived. "We ask our (letter) writers to be civil, even as public life increasing grows uncivil," states *The Mobile (Ala.) Register's* Web page.

Civility was apparently the last thing on the mind of one irate letter writer who didn't approve of the way his former girlfriend was raising their child. He was further incensed that he was being denied his free speech right to have his opinions on the subject published in the newspaper. The Southern Newspaper Association's *Bulletin* offered an explanation of why a free press doesn't mean people have the right to put anything they want in the newspaper. "That's not what free press means, of course. Free press means the press is free from government control. It doesn't mean that every crackpot with a grudge can use your newspaper to spread rumors, cast aspersions and distort facts. Lots of people think the media does that just fine without help from others."

Many newspapers want only original letters and will reject, mass mailings, form letters or those published elsewhere.

Some additional restrictions may also apply concerning political letters prior to an election. Endorsements or accusations involving candidates are usually not printed so close to an election that there is not enough time to print a response from the opposition.

Editors often prefer that readers share their ideas on subjects of public interest, and issues in the news. As a rule, most won't accept poetry, open letters, thank-you notes of a personal nature or letters to third parties. Seeking information about a long-lost relative who may have lived in the paper's coverage area is not an appropriate subject for letters to the editor. While in most cases unpublished letters can't be acknowledged, if after reviewing all the paper's guidelines you haven't seen your letter published within a week or two of sending it, call the editor for an explanation. Besides giving your name and when the letter was mailed, explain what it was about.

Most papers will edit letters for brevity, taste, grammar and clarity. *The Columbus (Ga.) Ledger-Enquirer* even corrects "mistakes of fact," according to its Web site.

While the majority of letters are still sent by U.S. mail, many newspapers are accepting them by a variety of other means. For example, the *Atlanta Constitution* editorial page provides prospective writers with a post office box address, fax number and e-mail address as well as a telephone number for calling in letters. (Most policies require submissions to be signed by their writers, but exceptions are made for e-mails and other electronic transmissions.)

Some newspapers will also allow a photo of the writer to be published along with the letter. In such cases photos should be submitted at the same time.

Be sure to make it clear when a letter to a newspaper editor is not for publication. Sometimes letters or invitations are intended to be of a more personal nature, but the assumption may be that the information is for public release unless otherwise noted. The brother of a murder victim wrote a letter criticizing the newspaper for not doing an update on the case five years after the killing and the letter ended up on that paper's editorial page. The writer called later to say his letter was a suggestion to the news staff and was not meant for publication. Also be clear about whether a telephone number or e-mail address is intended to be included in the text to be printed.

• **Guest columns.** These are often longer letters on a particular subject. They are usually written and submitted by someone who has expertise in the topic or whose job or position lends credibility to the opinions expressed. Sometimes newspapers will seek out local experts to write columns about issues in their fields. These can be anyone from government spokespersons to area doctors or social workers.

Guest columns, of from 500 to 800 words, are also usually accepted from anyone who has a well thought-out argument that takes more space to explore or explain than what is customarily available in the letters area. Writers should specify on their copy that they are submitting the piece for consideration as a column rather than a letter. A paragraph about the writer (place of residence, occupation, etc.) should also be included that provides the reader with some idea of the authority with which the essay is written. Some papers also prefer that photos be submitted to run with columns. Larger papers pay writers whose columns are selected for publication. The *Charlotte (N.C.) Observer*, for instance, pays freelancers a fifty-dollar fee. Commentary articles should be typed, not handwritten. Enclose a self-addressed, stamped envelope if you want your material returned.

• **Reader response forms.** This is another way of soliciting public opinion from those who have something to say but who may be reluctant to compose a letter from scratch. The forms appear on some editorial pages regularly to pose a question on an issue of public interest. They can be filled out and mailed in and, like letters, usually require a name, address and phone number. This can be an effective way to conduct a quick poll of the community on a hot issue.

Such was the case with the Cracker Trail controversy.

The issue involved the naming of a new elementary school that was located along the historical east-west route used by cattle drivers in Central Florida in the 1800s. County school board members thought the name "Cracker Trail Elementary School" was a natural. But they made their decision without realizing the problem the black community had with the word "cracker." It was considered a derogatory term, used to describe a white racist. Some members of the community raised the concern that such a name would stigmatize black children who attended the school. After being so informed, the school board rescinded its decision on the name. But that action didn't sit well with others in the community who thought the original name was appropriate. Many of them were proud to claim to be descendants of crackers. They argued that the old Florida cowboys had gotten their name from the sound their whips made while moving cattle along the trail, and had nothing to do with racism. The newspaper published a reader response coupon on the question and received hundreds of replies. The overwhelming majority supported the Cracker Trail name. Based on that response, school board members reinstated the school name. The final decision certainly didn't make everyone happy, but it was based on a consensus of community opinion that the newspaper helped reveal.

- **Street interviews.** Rather than wait for readers to send in their thoughts, this time-tested method of soliciting opinion involves having news staff members actually leave the comfort of the newsroom and ask people face-to-face for their opinions on an issue. Because respondents do not have the time to consider their answers as they would if they were writing to the paper, the questions are usually simply stated and responses are short, often only a sentence or two.

- **Voice-mail surveys.** These can range from questions focusing on a single issue to a "Sound-off" feature that allows the caller to comment on anything. Readers are asked to call a number to voice their comments, which are recorded on anything from a sophisticated digital system to a simple answering machine. The comments are then transcribed and published. In many cases, callers are not required to leave their names. This means, however, that all comments must be screened and not everything will make it to the printed page. The anonymity this feature allows can provide the newspaper with a broad view because it can include the opinions of people who may not comment if they had to write down their thoughts or sign their names. The validity of the poll, however, can be suspect because there is nothing to keep the same person from calling more than once to register an opinion.

• **Telephone Polls.** Because of the expense and time involved, these are not usually conducted on a regular basis by most newspapers. When they are commissioned, they tend to focus on specific issues. Polls typically crop up during Presidential election years, but can also be periodically conducted on issues such as crime and the environment. Phone polls solicit opinion from a fraction of the general population to provide a sample that represents what everyone is thinking (statistically speaking). Poll participants are usually chosen at random.

• **Editorial cartoons.** Newspapers that can't afford to pay their own editorial cartoonist often buy their cartoons from the papers do have those resources. The best cartoonists—most of them based at large metropolitan newspapers—are able to syndicate their creations because they have the ability to express an opinion strongly or make a point in a single image with few words and in a way that makes readers think or laugh or do both. That's not an easy task.

Some newspapers will accept guest cartoons from local readers, and fledgling political cartoonists may be able to get a break and land a regular job drawing for small newspapers. (One weekly ran regular submissions from a prison inmate. Art was a part of his rehabilitation program.) In most cases, however, readers will find much easier ways to express their opinions than through political cartooning.

Commentary tips

To sum up, here are some tips about giving your community newspaper a piece of your mind:

- Keep it brief. Try to keep it to a page (double-spaced) or about 150 to 250 words if possible.

- Type letters or write legibly. *The Herald-Sun* (Durham, N.C.), for example, notes, "Typewritten letters will receive priority."

- Include a phone number. Not only is this a requirement for verification at most newspapers, but it also provides the editor with a way to contact you if some clarification is needed on a handwritten letter or response coupon.

- Don't make unsubstantiated accusations or rant. Strive for a straightforward, persuasive argument supported by the facts.

- For faster sorting, put the words "Letter to the editor" or "Editorial Page" on the envelope.

- Stick to issues that are in the news.

- Reserve thanks or commendations for people or institutions that do more than their customary duties. Too often writers want to use the letters column to compliment someone for simply doing their job and it comes off sounding too much like a free plug for a business. That should be paid advertising.

• Don't expect or demand that your letter or other written response be printed without editing. Everything that goes into the newspaper has to go through at least one editor whose job is to make sure the piece conforms to the particular newspaper's style and is free of errors. There are times when a sloppy or careless editor will accidentally do something that changes the meaning of the submission or cuts out an important word or phrase, but often an editor's sharp eye will catch and correct something that could have caused embarrassment to the writer had it been printed.

• Customize your letter to a particular paper. Many editors won't accept a letter that is being sent to every media outlet in the area.

14. NEWS OF RECORD

A mere chronicle of observed events will produce only journalism; combined with a sensitive memory, it can produce art.

Hale Brunet
Writer, educator
1983

One of the primary purposes of a local newspaper is to chronicle the milestones in the lives of the people in its community, everything from birth announcements to obituaries, and hopefully some noteworthy events in between.

In many cases these personal items are submitted to the paper. People who provide this information on a regular basis should contact the editor or news clerk, who types or scans them, to ask about any special requirements for submission. The following is a rundown of some of the types of news of record items submitted and the way most newspapers like to see them. Keep in mind that such news can appear in different parts of the newspaper and be handled by a variety of editors.

• **Birth announcements.** Often a hospital will submit these to the hometown newspaper based on information supplied by the parents. Papers may also accept these releases from families. The information

118

usually includes: names and hometown of the parents, names and hometowns of the maternal grandparents (mother's parents) and paternal grandparents (father's parents), name of the newborn, length and weight, and date and place of birth. Other items that may be accepted for publication are the names of siblings (brothers and sisters) of the newborn and other local relatives.

• **Professions of faith.** This includes various church accomplishments such as baptisms and confirmations that are a significant part of a person's religious life. In most cases churches submit this information, but the person involved may also provide it.

• **Education awards and recognition**. This would include lists of names such as honor rolls, which are usually sent by schools. Sending honor rolls in a digital form such as an e-mail file makes it much easier on news clerks who have to otherwise type long lists of names, and makes it more likely that the published list will be free of typos.

• **Engagements, weddings and anniversaries.** Individuals or families submit these items. Most newspapers have standard forms that explain what information is needed and how it should be presented. (See the examples in Appendix C.)

Photos are also often used, but newspaper policies vary as to who should appear in the pictures. Some papers stick to an old tradition that only the bride-to-be is shown in engagement photos, while others allow the prospective bride and groom to appear. Paid announcements, which are the only kind some newspapers accept, can include just about anything and anyone desired.

Engagement announcements should identify the parents of the couple and their hometowns as well as information about the couple. Announcements usually mention where the bride-elect and groom-elect went to school and where each is employed. The date of the wedding, if set, should be included or at least an indication of when it will occur. Example: "A fall wedding is planned." While most engagements are set well in advance of the actual nuptials, submit the announcement no more than six months and not less than two weeks before the wedding.

Wedding announcements are traditionally longer than the engagement releases. Many newspapers allow long descriptions of the bride's attire and flowers and the ceremony itself. Other information should include the names and hometowns of the wedding party (father and mother of the bride and groom, maid of honor, best man, ushers, ring bearer, flower girl and those responsible for the guest book and other duties. One published wedding report even listed a job for the cousin of the bride. He carried the pen the couple used to sign the marriage license). Where the couple plan to honeymoon, and where they intend to reside after the trip, are also usually included in the published announcement.

Like thank-you notes to those who gave wedding gifts, wedding announcements are too often put off until after the ceremony and honeymoon, and may not make the news until a month or longer after the event. Some newspapers limit the time after a wedding when a free announcement can be submitted. *The LaGrange Daily News* in Georgia has a policy that wedding announcements can be submitted no later than two weeks after the ceremony.

Because the details of the ceremony and the people involved should already be known before the wedding, submit the announcement to the paper prior to the event. However, make sure to emphasize the date of the wedding because it would not do for the newspaper to publish news about how the ceremony went before it has even taken place.

Anniversary announcements are usually the shortest in this category and sometimes include only a photo of the couple and a caption. Some papers encourage couples to submit two photos, a current one and one that was taken on their wedding day. Information accompanying the photos should state the date of the marriage and may also include details of the anniversary party and even how the couple met. Policies vary on which anniversaries are accepted for publication. Some only publish announcements of 50 years or more, which really is news in an age of soaring divorce rates. (Totaling the years from two or more marriages does not count.) *The Sun Sentinel* of Ft. Lauderdale, Fla., for example, offers free anniversary announcements only to local couples that have "earned it." That means those who have been married at least half a century, according to that paper's view. *The Gainesville (Ga.) Times*, on the other hand, accepts anniversary announcements of 20 years or more.

Anniversary information is usually published free of charge by local newspapers. However, some print media companies looking for revenue wherever they can find it, charge a fee for such announcements, and an additional charge for photos. Even if large papers require fees for publishing these items in their metro editions, they still may print them for free in a zoned edition that serves your neighborhood in an outlying part of the paper's market.

- **Military service news.** This includes information on local people who have joined the service, completed basic training, have been deployed, promoted in rank or have received awards or have otherwise been recognized. The Hometown News Service, which is the US military's public relations division, supplies much of this information. News releases are sent to newspapers based on the place of permanent residence listed by a recruit or serviceperson.

- **Court records.** Almost anything filed at a courthouse, unless sealed by a judge or exempted by state law, is considered a public record. Civil documents include such things as deed transfers, small claims case filings and domestic lawsuits. Criminal documents include the disposition of various law violations ranging from charges of drunk drinking to first-degree murder. These items are usually gathered by reporters or news clerks from databases made available to the public by law enforcement agencies or the clerks of courts. Newspaper policies vary on what information, and how much of it, is routinely published.

• **Permits, zoning notices and inspection reports.** Building permits and results of health inspection reports compiled by a county or city government may be regularly reported by a newspaper as a public service. Notices of proposed zoning changes are published as news stories when deemed significant, although local or state laws often require them to be printed as paid legal advertising.

• **Obituaries and funeral notices.** What's the difference? Obituary information is most often obtained from the funeral homes involved in making final arrangements. Funeral notice information is usually obtained from the funeral home or directly from the family and often contains additional information other than what is included in a standard obituary. Another difference between the two traditionally has been that obituaries are printed free of charge by the newspaper; funeral notices, also known as death notices, bereavement notices or memorials, are paid advertisements published in addition to the obituary. This has changed in recent years as some newspapers have begun charging for publishing obituaries. Pat MacDonald, publisher of The *MacDonald Classified Service*, estimates that 90 percent of all major newspapers now charge for obits. Often that fee is billed to the funeral home, which then includes the cost in the overall funeral expenses paid by the family. Many newspapers offer the first few lines of an obituary free, which contain the basic death information, but require payment for additional lines with further details.

Obituaries consist of biographical accounts of a deceased person's life. The standard obituary contains the name, address, age and complete date of death of the deceased. The year is included because many obituaries are clipped from the paper and saved by the family and others for many years.

The place of death is usually mentioned as well as the place and date of birth. Some newspapers allow the publication of the names of immediate family members who preceded the deceased in death. The late newspaper editor Janelou Buck of The *News-Sun* of Sebring, Fla. wouldn't hear of such a thing, though. She would rhetorically ask, "Whose funeral is this anyway?" Such information, however, is often helpful to those who in later years are doing genealogy research.

Information about the deceased, such as education, occupations, military service, church and club memberships and awards or honors should be included. Survivors (living relatives) of the deceased's immediate family are listed. Policies vary as to who qualifies as a survivor. Most newspapers list the number of surviving grandchildren and great-grandchildren, but will not name them. Nor will they name the deceased's surviving in-laws, fiancées, cousins, nieces, nephews, or "special friends."

The times and dates of the visitation and funeral are included, as are the names of any pastors who will be officiating at the funeral and the names of the pallbearers. The names and addresses of any church or organizations where memorial contributions can be sent should be listed, and the name of the funeral home in charge of the arrangements. The cause of death is usually not mentioned in the standard free obituary, but it can be included in the notice if for some reason the family wants it publicized.

When having an obituary sent by the funeral home to a hometown paper in another state or city, make sure the local connection is clearly stated. An editor may assume there is some good reason why an effort is being made to have information on an out-of-town death published in the local paper. However, unless the obituary notice specifically notes that the deceased was a former resident of the paper's coverage area, or that survivors live there, he may question the justification for allotting space for the "foreign" obit.

Just as people are being urged to plan for the financing of their funerals in advance, thought should be given to providing information for their future obituaries. Grieving family members understandably can find it difficult to recall the entire life experiences of a loved one soon after death, yet the obituary information must be provided for publication at least a day or two before the funeral. It is not uncommon for distraught family members to even forget to include some names of the deceased's surviving relatives when assisting the funeral home in preparing an obit.

News-Sun editor Janelou Buck, who worked on tens of thousands of obituaries during her long newspaper career, wanted to make sure her own obituary was worded in a way that reflected how she wanted to be remembered. She wrote down the information, which contained items neither her closest friends nor family members may have thought of later. And the paper used it at the appropriate time.

Inventor Alfred Nobel reportedly had a chance to do something most of us never will. He had the opportunity to read his obituary in 1888, eight years before his death. Nobel's brother had died, but due to a mix-up at the paper, it was Alfred Nobel's demise that was being reported, and he didn't appreciate the apparent legacy he was leaving behind. Because of his invention of dynamite and its use in warfare, Nobel was referred to as a "merchant of death." That view of how his life would be perceived after he was gone reportedly inspired him to establish funding for the Nobel prizes and secured his legacy as a man of peace.

It may seem morbid for people to think about their own deaths when they are still alive and well. But who is more qualified to sum up the significant events and accomplishments of our own lives than we are?

It is also a good idea to have at least one decent photo of yourself or a loved one in a place that is easily accessible. Family members often want to publish a photograph of the deceased with an obit of a relative, but the only image they may be able to find of Uncle Fred is a blurry Polaroid of him wearing an old flannel shirt and baseball cap, and sitting at a kitchen table strewn with cigarettes and beer cans. Maybe that is the way he wanted to be remembered—or the family thought he should be remembered—but most of us would want to leave a little more dignified image behind.

Public information

Even though news of record information is available for public inspection, some people are not interested in having it publicized in the local newspaper. It's not unusual to have calls to newspapers asking them not to publish a police report that tells of the arrest of a family member or a deed transfer that reveals the sale price of their property. Even a marriage license listing can bring objections because a fiancée doesn't want her age known, or there is some other sensitive situation involved. In one case, a bride-to-be told an editor she didn't want people to know that she and groom were not already married, and in another the happy couple said they didn't want their relatives to know anything about it.

In many cases, however, the reason given as to why public records should not be made public in the newspaper is simply, "It's nobody's damn business what I do!"

15. THAT'S NOT MY DEPARTMENT

*My friends think that all radio
stations look like WKRP in
Cincinnati. And I'm sure they think
newspapers are put out by a half
dozen people with typewriters.*

James W. Wesley Jr.
Media executive
1994

When school groups tour a newspaper plant the guides often highlight
the newsroom as the heart and soul of the publishing enterprise. More
often than not, however, the children are more impressed with the multi-
story and thunderously loud equipment found in the pressroom.

While the reporters and editors who produce the news may be the
best-known newspaper employees in the eyes of the public, there are
several people in other departments who play vital roles in putting the
daily or weekly product together. Actually it is hard to say which is the
most important. Without the circulation department the news would
not get to the reader's homes or to the newsstands. Without the
compositors the stories, photos and ads would not make it onto the
pages. Those pages couldn't be printed without the pressroom crew. If
not for the advertising managers and sales representatives, the publisher

might not be able to afford to pay anyone. And if not for the bookkeepers in the business office, nobody would be able to track where the money is coming or going.

Anyone who submits items to the paper, subscribes to it, or reads a copy on occasion may have to deal with any of these departments at some time. It can come in handy to know who to seek out to resolve a problem or answer a question. Such knowledge can certainly help avoid the runaround associated with being passed from phone extension to extension. Usually, the receptionist who answers the phone or greets visitors should know where to direct a call—if you are fortunate enough to have a live person answer your call and not an automated telephone attendant. In either case, already knowing a little about the following departments can save a little time and trouble and help expand your understanding of your local newspaper. Here is a quick tour:

- **Advertising.** These are the people who sell the big display advertisements and little classified (line) ads that appear on various pages of the paper. Ad revenue accounts for the majority of the financial support of the operation of the newspaper, which could not survive in its current form from the money paid for the product by the consumer. This department handles items published in the paper as paid notices, which can include anything from garage sale announcements to funeral notices.

The ad department might be further divided into retail and classified divisions. The retail side deals with businesses such as stores and other regular advertisers who pay for the display ads that can range from a 1 by 1 inch block of type to a full page—or even several pages—with words, pictures and illustrations.

Classified ads, commonly known as want ads, usually consist of small blocks of type and are often used to publicize things such as job openings, items for sale, services for hire, garage sales, and lost pets.

A class of paid advertising that resembles news copy is often referred to as "advertorial" (a combination of advertising and editorial). Touting anything from business opportunities to new "breakthroughs" in the science of health or cosmetics, these ads may even include photos and headlines. To help ensure that readers don't confuse paid placements with news reports, they are often set in a different typestyle than the regular news copy, and are usually tagged with a line identifying them as advertisements.

A newspaper's marketing efforts may also be operated from the advertising department.

• **Bookkeeping.** This department handles the internal accounting for the newspaper and its employees but also may be in charge of billing customers for advertisements. People who have been billed incorrectly for their ad or subscription may save some time by going directly to bookkeeping with their inquires. A controller or business manager usually heads the department.

• **Circulation.** Delivering the newspaper to homes, newsstands, news racks and stores is the primary responsibility of the circulation department. It may also be in charge of the mailroom or packaging center that is responsible for inserting advertising sections and preparing the paper for delivery after it comes off the press. The mailroom also prepares papers for mailing to customers outside the delivery area.

Problems with missed deliveries should be directed to the circulation staff or manager. Circulation departments also are often responsible for keeping back issues of the paper, so a request might be made here for an edition that was missed or an old issue needed for research purposes.

• **Composing.** This department traditionally gets the copy and photos from the newsroom and the ads from advertising and puts together (composes) the pages, based on page designs provided by the editors.

Many composing departments are experiencing dramatic changes as papers switch over to electronic pagination of pages. Instead of cutting paper on which type has been set, coating the copy with hot wax, and pasting the stories on a paper sheet the size of a newspaper page, computers are being used in many places to electronically make up the pages on a screen. They are then sent to printers, film processors, or directly to the press units.

Typically, most readers and news release writers won't have much direct contact with composing.

• **Editorial.** The news department or newsroom is where the editors, reporters, and photographers work. Many larger papers subdivide their editorial departments into separate divisions responsible for local news (city desk), state, national and world news, sports, lifestyles, photos, editorial page, etc.

• **Pressroom.** The pressroom is where the ink meets the newsprint. The pressroom usually doesn't have much contact with the public, but if you find you're leaving black fingerprints around the house after reading the newspaper and call in a complaint, it is the press foreman or manager who will most likely be asked to make some adjustments to reduce the rub-off. The pressroom may also be responsible if readers find the type on one or more of the newspaper pages is too dark or too light to read.

• **Publisher.** The publisher is responsible for overseeing all the departments and is the person to see when you can't resolve problems with the other departments. The name of the publisher usually appears at the top of the editorial page and in the masthead often found on page 2.

The publisher, not the editor, is the real boss of the whole operation, so if you want to talk to the top man—or woman—you need to direct your call there. On a small paper the same person may be both the editor and publisher.

• **Systems**. This is a fairly recent addition from the traditional departmental structure of the newspaper. The systems department, which may also be referred to as technical support, data processing or by a variety of other names, is responsible for the computers and other electronic equipment upon which newspapers have become dependent in recent years. Some smaller papers may have a member of one of the other departments serve as a systems person or may have an outside consultant perform this function. If the newspaper has an Internet homepage, its Webmaster may be assigned this duty. Public contacts with systems can come from those who want to electronically transmit news copy, photos or ads to the newspaper.

This actually may be the most important department because, as in many businesses, newspapers have become dependant on technology. And when computer systems go down much of the work throughout the entire organization comes to a screeching halt.

16. TOURING AN EDITOR'S WASTEBASKET

Everybody gets so much informa-
tion all day long that they lose their
common sense.

Gertrude Stein
Writer
1946

What follows is a sampling of the many pieces of mail and faxes that don't make the cut for publication with a short explanation for their rejection. Keep in mind that this is a small fraction of the hundreds of bits of correspondence that come across the news desk every day.

E-mailers in recent years have joined the many businesses, individuals and organizations that spend a lot of time and resources sending out releases with little, if any, chance they will be accepted for publication. Many publicity people at these companies or public institutions apparently just need to show that they have met their quota of releases sent to the media. The end result of whether that information has actually been printed for human consumption is apparently not as important to them. Releases of "general" interest are often sent to every newspaper listed in a database without regard to how much actual interest they may be to the readership of any particular circulation area. Technology, i.e., the fax machine and computer modems, also play a part in the increase in distribution of wastebasket fodder. It is easier and cheaper to distribute news releases automatically to everyone at once by way of an automated mailing list rather than by addressing and attaching postage to individual envelops. Editors are starting to get so many junk faxes and e-mails that the words "Important Facsimile" on the cover sheet or "Urgent E-mail" in the subject line are becoming contradictions in terms.

While reading the following items, remember that the fate of a release will often be decided in the first few seconds of consideration either by an editor, news clerk or some other editorial department staffer. This quick subjective judgment will vary based on the location, size and readership of the publication involved. In the cases of these actual releases, I was editing a paper in the foothills of western North Carolina. (Names of most of the submitters have been omitted or altered.) Rejection doesn't necessarily mean the item would not have been of interest to any of the newspaper's readers, but that it just didn't have enough local appeal to compete for news space with other items at the particular time it was rejected. Remember too, that the needs of newspapers for certain material can change. For example, when our paper began publishing an automotive section, submissions on new car models that were of limited use previously became much more in demand. But for the most part, the majority of items submitted still don't make the grade. Newspapers discard from 50 to 95 percent of the items they receive. This tour will give you some idea why.

- "FOR IMMEDIATE RELEASE

Daytona Beach, Fl.—The largest combined car show and swap meet in the southeast will be held in the infield at the Daytona International Speedway..."

It would have to be pretty spectacular indeed to entice our area readers to jet hundreds of miles for a car show.

- "FOR IMMEDIATE RELEASE

HAIRSYLISTS OFFER TIPS TO
PUMP UP THE VOLUME IN YOUR HAIR

MINNEAPOLIS—Fine, thin hair is a perplexing beauty problem for many women. Fortunately, getting volume back into the hair can be easy."

This may very well be a perplexing problem for some readers but it doesn't stack up on the publishing priority list when compared to local news releases, community social issues and basic human needs such as food, shelter and medical care. This is also an example of a large percentage of the items sent to newspapers and other media that consists of advertising doing a bad impersonation of news. There is a difference between business/consumer news and attempts at free advertising.

- "For immediate release:

WASHINGTON, D.C.—A just-released national survey on attitudes on environmental policy shows that most Americans support new approaches to environmental protection, but not necessarily extensive federal regulations."

Not all the lobbying in this country is directed at elected officials in Washington, state capitals and city halls. Many times, groups with a variety of names—often the words Independent, American, National and Institute are included in the titles—bombard newspapers with opinion pieces in hopes of getting them published on the editorial pages either as guest columns, or through having some of the information incorporated into editorials. Depending on the sources cited, editors are often suspicious about the results of surveys or studies that may be conducted by groups intent on getting results that conform to what they want to find. Much more of this information usually is available than could be accommodated on daily opinion pages, so editors can show a great deal of discretion in determining what to use to present a balanced presentation of various issues. Again, most papers will give preference to local letters and columns that address issues of immediate or general concern to the newspaper's readers, or pieces that provide an opposing view to one previously presented.

• "WASHINGTON, D.C.—Is your medication too expensive for your budget? If so, information in a new booklet might help."

People who see a "consumer interest" news item with a Washington, D.C. dateline or address often assume that the group offering information is a federal government agency. In many cases it is not, even though the information being offered is available from the government for free. In this particular case, this group's release offers the booklet for $3 to cover the cost of postage and handling. I'm not insinuating that any of these news items are not legitimate or may not be of interest to some readers. I'm just trying to point out some of what is included in the news release mix and the reasons why at least one newspaper editor decided to pass on them.

• "For release: IMMEDIATE

RALEIGH, N.C.—Another deadbeat parent on the second Governor's Crackdown for Children '10 most wanted' poster has been arrested. Michael John Noname, who owes his daughter in Other County almost $40,000 in back child support, was arrested Aug. 2 in Mississippi after agents received a tip on his whereabouts."

This guy apparently had the bad judgment to welsh on his child support payments and the bad luck to do it during an election year when the governor just happened to be in the midst of a high profile crackdown on "deadbeat parents." The governor, however, had the bad luck of faxing his press release to a paper that had already run a local story on overdue child support in its own county, and was not interested in giving the incumbent candidate more exposure than he already gets from wire service stories on the state page.

• "IMMEDIATE RELEASE

SALISBURY, N.C.—Mr. Freeze's walk-in coolers now have the big responsibility of keeping food and beverages cool at the Carolina Panthers' new Ericsson Stadium in Charlotte, North Carolina. Their walk-in refrigeration equipment, which was recently installed, was the only refrigeration storage equipment chosen for installation in the facility."

What a coincidence! I had a call just the other day from a reader who was desperate to know what type of refrigeration equipment was being used in the stadium. Yeah, right.

- "FOR IMMEDIATE RELEASE

WINSTON-SALEM, N.C.—Sounds like a trivial problem, but it has plagued medical researchers for years now: How do you get an accurate reading of a mouse's blood pressure?"

I don't know, but I am quite certain the rest of this three-page release will tell me how the brilliant research assistant professors in the department of orthopedic surgery at a particular medical center were able to solve this problem. Interesting, but often not interesting enough to bump an honor roll listing or a column of military service news from a local newspaper.

- "RALEIGH—North Carolina's first infestation of tropical soda apple, a damaging weed that overtakes crop land and adjacent native areas, has been identified in a Samson County pasture."

Yawn. Let us know when that soda stuff gets within 100 miles or so of our coverage area.

- "DEAR CORPORATE LEADERS:

What does your corporation have, that it has not yet been allowed to acquire by our heavenly father? God has given this humble prophet this message for all corporation, business and spiritual leaders in the world today! Awaken! I have instructed my servant "Tex" to send this letter to this world's business leaders, spiritual leaders, and political leaders in this world today!"

This was one of my favorites because it had the words "FREE GIFTS" stamped on the envelope. Anyone who thinks they have to entice an editor with freebies for news coverage usually doesn't have much worth reporting.

• "NASHVILLE, Tenn.—National Outdoor Products announced today that it is a winner of the prestigious 1995 First Place SPARC (Supplier Performance Award by Retail Category) Award. The award is based on a poll of the key merchandising executives in the $264 billion discount retailing industry conducted by *Rockbottom Store News*."

Congratulations, but you were beat out in our paper by a local daycare center's employee of the month.

• "Consumers assume that all vacuum cleaners are basically alike … "

I smell an ad.

• "BROOKLYN, N.Y.—A smart new perfume company has jumped on the time-management bandwagon to help busy women and men eliminate one time-consuming chore from their schedules—shopping for perfume and cologne."

Shouldn't they have a Nobel Prize category for such contributions to mankind?

• "Ever since the revival in popularity of braided hair styles, people have been looking for a quicker way to braid hair. The answer to their prayers has finally arrived.…"

Looks like I was too quick to make that Nobel Prize nomination.

• "SPIRITUAL CLONING

Cloning—Am I writing this article or is my clone writing it? Are you reading this article or is your clone reading it, or are you the clone?"
Actually, I would have published this one but, you see, my evil clone got hold of it and trashed it before I could do anything with it.

• "NEW CHEWING GUM INCREASES THE PERFORMANCE OF YOUR BRAIN

BRAIN GUM contains, PS (Phosphatidylserine), and by chewing BRAIN GUM you can improve the performance of your brain. Over 34 clinical studies show that PS can improve your concentration, increase memory, recall and learning."

The first thing you will figure out is how dumb it was to pay 42 cents for a stick of gum. This is one of many "amazing scientific breakthroughs" that are an attempt to advertise the sale of a product.

• "REVOLUTIONARY DIAPER FIXES TODDLER LEAK PROBLEM IN TIME FOR SUMMER POOL OPENINGS

Richard Nixon hated them. They drove Henry Kissinger crazy. Bill Clinton despises them. Leaks, of course. Now, with the approach of pool opening days, added to the list of leak-haters are managers of public swimming pools, concerned about toddlers with leaky diapers messing up their wading pools."

I really don't make these things up, folks.

Even in this digital age, newspaper editors handle a lot of pieces of paper. You've just gotten some idea why a great majority of them will wind up in a garbage can or recycling bin.

17. BROADCAST NEWS

*We hear a lot about what televi-
sion has done to the attention span of
the American public. We should
worry at least as much about what
the attentions span of the American
public has done to television.*

John Leonard
Social critic
1997

The traditional broadcast or electronic media—radio and television—
provide limited opportunities for community news promotion compared
to newspapers. Airtime just isn't as plentiful as newsprint news hole. That
doesn't mean that news releases are never accepted or used by the electronic media. Public Service Announcements (PSAs) are regularly aired.
Local cable television channels and small community radio stations are
also potential sources of good press. But due to the nature of broadcast,
the chances of getting a news release published in print are far greater than
having it used on TV or radio.

TV

A county housing authority that needed to generate public support to develop a low-income residential project was able to convince a local television station to do a story on the effort. Authority members anticipated that a three or four-minute segment on the evening news would give a boost to their fund-raising endeavors. When a storage room fire destroyed much of the other material scheduled for that night's program, however, the housing story received the full twenty-three minutes of airplay available. That one night's exposure enabled the organization to raise enough community support to establish the project.

Because of popular viewing habits, television can offer a tremendous opportunity for publicizing an event, but like show business in general, it is not easy to break into. Newspapers traditionally cover most local stories that have news or feature value, while television affiliates usually are based in metropolitan areas and focus on major news stories with visual appeal. Despite budgets generous enough to afford helicopters and the latest in weather forecasting equipment, TV does have its limitations. The news staffs are often small (at least compared to metro daily newspapers) the deadlines are tight and action sequences are in demand. These factors can complicate and frustrate news release efforts because TV news directors have to be selective about what they present to their viewers.

NBC affiliate WPSD TV, for example, accepts news releases and public service announcements by e-mail, but doesn't air everything received. "When selecting news stories, we hold editorial meetings twice a day and discuss various story possibilities," assignment manager Andrea Underwood notes in explaining the general procedure of determining what gets on the air. "We try to choose items that most of our viewers will find interesting or helpful in some way. The public service announcements we choose to air are usually big events that have the potential to attract a large number of people."

When submitting a news release to a TV station, note any visual opportunities that exist. When possible, tell your story in a personal way by using real people engaged in an activity. The common thread in all media promotion—whether it is to be read, heard or viewed—is bringing out the human-interest aspect. A piece on a fund-raising event for the local animal shelter, for example, will be more effective, and have a better chance of getting air play, if some film of abandoned pets is included. You don't have to be a Hollywood producer to think in terms of "good television."

But unless you have exclusive footage of a natural disaster or other breaking news event, don't submit home videos with the expectation that they will be aired. While a television production is expensive, a professionally shot and edited promotional piece is usually the only way to approach the quality standards needed for broadcast.

Attracting a professional camera crew from the local station is your best bet. However, some precautions are in order if you are fortunate enough to set up a shoot. TV reporters like to get quotes to add color to their stories as much as print journalists, but people being interviewed for broadcast have to be much more aware of what they say and how they say it. Television and radio people can report only the barest essentials of a story so they are looking for succinct answers to one of two questions. As many successful politicians have learned, thinking in terms of "sound bites" is often the most effective means of getting their message across in the electronic media. Interview subjects should avoid time-consuming details, rambling explanations and complicated responses because many times these statements will be abruptly clipped or not used at all. A two-hour television interview, for instance, might be slotted for only thirty seconds of airtime. Time—especially television time—is money. When pitching a story or submitting one, think in terms of what can be presented in about half a minute or less.

Cable TV time may be more accessible to organizations and individuals because of the large number of open slots per week. Local cable operators air public announcements with greater frequency and their production requirements may not be as stringent as stations affiliated with networks. Survey responses from more than two hundred cable systems revealed that while only one-fourth had news departments, half were interested in receiving video news releases. The majority of those cable operators preferred localized public service announcements (PSAs) to national items. Charter Communications, for example, broadcasts PSAs on its government access channels. Announcements can be faxed and should contain a heading and no more than seven lines of type with thirty-two characters per line. As with any free media posting, there is no guarantee that the news release will be broadcast.

Just as with newspapers, people dealing with TV news should respect deadlines. The most common television news affiliate deadlines are 10:30 a.m., 4:30 p.m. and 9:30 p.m. Cable news deadlines vary.

Expect any interview you do to be edited and prepare for that eventuality. Decide in advance on a few key points, rehearse your comments, state your key points at the beginning of each response and repeat them to provide emphasis and increase chances they will make it into the edited broadcast. The University of Wisconsin in Madison's communications department advises developing a SOCO—a Single Overriding Communications Object—when preparing for a broadcast interview. The most important point you want to make should be weaved into your comments as much as possible. Videotaping practice sessions and reviewing them is a good way to fine-tune your on-air presentation.

Here are some additional tips for doing a broadcast interview:

- **Repeat the question.** This gives you a chance to think while forming a short, positive and accurate answer. It also helps the viewers in case they missed the question the first time.

- **Don't repeat the question**. There are always exceptions to the rules and this is one of them. Be careful not to repeat negative words in a question that could appear to taint your response. Reporters can frame questions to bring out the conflict in a story because conflict is news. To avoid fanning controversy, state your position in positive terms.

• **Tell the truth.** Follow the same advice as in print interviews. Be truthful and do not speculate about information you don't know.

• **Do not give personal opinions**. Any public comments broadcast by a spokesperson for an organization are likely to be assumed by viewers to also be the position of the organization he is representing. As William Strunk Jr. and E.B. White note in "The elements of Style," "We all have opinions about almost everything, and the temptation to toss them in is great. To air one's views gratuitously, however, is to imply that the demand for them is brisk, which may not be the case, and which, in any event, may not be relevant to the discussion."

• **Say the reporter's name**. Using the interviewer's name not only helps establish a friendly atmosphere, but also increases the chances that what you say won't be cut from the edited version.

• **Think fast. Talk slowly.** Take your time in responding to questions. Your answers will come across much clearer to the viewer and make better sense.

• **Speak to your audience.** Remember to whom you are talking. It's not the reporter with the pad and microphone, but the thousands and maybe millions of viewers who will eventually hear what you say.

Radio

Radio stations have smaller staffs than television and newspapers— often only one person serving as a general assignment reporter—so they have to concentrate their resources on covering only major, hard news. Many radio stations use syndicated news services that highlight the day's top stories from around the world. Most news directors, however, do find a spot for local news and events. Interviews with local news sources are most often taped for later and repeated broadcasts but they can also be aired live. The preceding broadcast interview tips apply to radio as well as television. Deadlines for radio newscasts are flexible throughout the day.

Radio spots require tightly written pieces. You should be able to read a 20-word announcement aloud in about 10 seconds at a normal speaking pace. Spots can also be prepared for 15 and 30-second lengths but the longer the piece, the less chance that air time will be available. If the item is approaching 100 words it is too long. Samples of radio spots are included in Appendix B.

PSAs

A PSA (Public Service Announcement) is any unpaid notice that promotes voluntary, government or non-profit organizations, events, activities, services or programs. The key for a PSA, according to Federal Communications Commission (FCC) guidelines, is that it serves "community interests." The following are general instructions for preparing and submitting PSAs but remember that stations may have their own specific requirements:

- **Presentation.** All information sent to broadcasters should be typed and double-spaced. Some stations prefer announcements to be typed in large capital letters.

- **Stick to the point.** Do not clutter PSAs with extraneous information such as annual reports. Send only relevant information.

- **Introduce yourself.** Send along a brief letter of introduction explaining the announcement. The letter should include the submitting organization's name and address, the contact name and a phone number in case the broadcaster needs additional information. Pointing out in this letter how the announcement serves the public interest can enhance the chances of it being used as a PSA.

• **Submit early.** Allow a lead-time of two to three weeks to give the broadcaster a chance to work the PSA into the schedule.

• **Target your message.** Tailor the PSA to the medium for which it is intended. For example, PSAs for radio should be written so they are easy to read and in simple language that can be easily understood by the casual listener. Remember that these are no longer the days of the "Fireside chat" where people are gathered around the radio intently hanging on every word of a broadcast. More likely they are driving, working or engaged in recreational activity as they listen to the broadcast.

• **Help out the announcer.** Use brief, one-sentence paragraphs. Separate clauses and uses ellipses (…) to give broadcasters an indication of where to pause in long sentences. Remember that the key is to clearly communicate your message, so do not use contractions or words that are difficult to pronounce. When you do have to include an unusual name or word, provide help by putting the phonetic spelling in parentheses immediately after the unfamiliar word.

• **Show appreciation.** A call or note of thanks—an all too rare occurrence in any media—is much appreciated and can enhance the organization's public relations.

• **Radio formats.** Radio stations usually prefer pre-taped announcements. The format, however, may vary so check with the local station before going to the trouble and expense of recording a PSA. The following is the PSA policy for WFAE 90.7FM, a public radio station located in Charlotte, N.C.:

WFAE 90.7fm strives to include PSAs from as many different sources as possible in the station's community calendar. The PSAs will focus on basic facts. No lengthy descriptions will be given. They will be edited to meet WFAE 90.7fm specifications. No phone numbers of organizations will be given over the air. Instead listeners will be encouraged to call WFAE 90.7fm for more information about events. If WFAE 90.7fm can use a PSA, it will be placed in a rotation with 10-25 other PSAs. WFAE 90.7fm does not guarantee the number of readings or times of day.

There are some items we cannot air because of the large number of PSAs we receive. Those include:

1. Informational announcements.

2. Any event that is not open to the public.

3. Your group's weekly or monthly meeting, except when a speaker of unusual local, regional or national prominence will be appearing.

4. Any solicitation for auditions.

5. Car washes, dinners, bake sales, attic sales, tournaments, or similar group fund raisers.

6. Events at your church or synagogue, except for significant concerts or lectures.

7. Any event that is sponsored by another radio station.

8. Any recorded material for PSAs.

Information sent to WFAE 90.7fm must arrive by mail, fax or e-mail at least two weeks before your event. Items will be considered for air if the following information is included:

1. Name of event and sponsoring organization

2. Date of event (with multi-day events, plays, etc., please include each individual performance date.

3. Time of event (on all performance dates.)

4. Street address of event.

5. Description of event

6. Phonetic pronunciation of unusual names.

7. Ticket or admission costs for event or for each performance.

8. Contact name and telephone.

TV formats. Television stations may accept both videotaped and written announcements. The written announcements will more likely be displayed on a community calendar. At WCYB, an NBC affiliate in Bristol, Va., video PSAs have to meet the station's requirements. Those that do get on the air are usually produced by national non-profit organizations.

The Internet

News releases can also be distributed worldwide on the Internet at little or no cost. When e-mailing, put the words "PRESS RELEASE" at the start of the subject line. Use regular text in the message body. Editors will not convert messages from MIME (Multipurpose Internet Mail Extensions).

Most services distribute press releases for a fee while others advertise free distribution. These services categorize releases by subject and target the distribution in that way. Unlike newspapers and other media where a judgment call is made on the information being submitted for publication, information posted on the free-flowing Internet often goes out unfiltered. This has resulted in what *Time* magazine referred to as a "rising tide of misinformation" in a story about online stock scams. Even the people behind the PR Web service, who claim to distribute as many as 150 releases a day, note that they "strongly believe in traditional distribution services" for news releases. They advise companies and organizations to augment their print and broadcast public relations efforts with postings on the Internet.

The following are tips for Web PR suggested in Rotary International's Public Relations Tool Kit. They are reprinted here with the permission of Phillips PR News:

• Make sure key information is available in several different formations in addition to HTML (Hyper Text Markup Language). Microsoft Word and WordPerfect are always good choices. You'll get extra public relations points if you make your press releases and other documents easily downloadable through an FTP (File Transfer Protocol) site.

• Do not e-mail large text or graphics files. This consumes too many resources. It's better to post them on the Web or make them downloadable via FTP.

• Make sure any streaming video is presented in a standard AVI (Audio Video Interleaved) format. The file should also meet compression standards for audio and video signals.

• Use lower bandwidths and smaller downloads to make data retrieval easier. Keep graphics small and simple.

• Use your Internet site to respond to information and requests through e-mail, interactive forms, surveys or chats.

• Get listed on as many different Internet search engines as possible.

Whether you target the Web, TV or radio for your electronic news release, don't forget the basic five questions that should be always be addressed in any submission: Who, What, When, Where and How.

ABOUT THE AUTHOR)

Richard V. Tuttell is the executive editor of a daily newspaper. He has written thousands of published articles during an award-winning journalism career that spans more than two decades. His professional experience has included stints as a reporter and editor at a variety of small community newspapers in the Southeastern United States, and 11 years with the New York Times Regional Newspaper Group. A graduate of Florida Technological University/The University of Central Florida with a Bachelor of Science degree in Political Science, he speaks often about community newspapers and for the past several years has organized and conducted a leadership class on media relations for Chamber of Commerce members. He lives with his wife in the Foothills of North Carolina.

APPENDIX A

Sample press release

(The following press release format is acceptable to most newspapers:)

CONTACT: (Name)   FOR IMMEDIATE RELEASE
                (Telephone)
                (Fax/e-mail)   (Date mailed)

Local student named International Genius Scholar

(CITY)—(Scholar's name), sponsored by the Civic Club of (city) was awarded an International Genius Scholarship for the 2002-03 school year. (Student's last name) plans to study at (university) in (city and country).

(Include scholar information here such as name of parents, hometown, educational background, other honors, study plans, civic activities, and achievements.)

(Last name) is only one of 100 students in the United States to receive the scholarship this year. (Name) will receive funds for travel, accommodations, tuition and fees to study abroad for one year.

The International Genius Scholarship is (explain the mission of the scholarship). It was established in (explain the background of the educational award and the sponsoring organization).

For more information on the scholarship or the Civic Club contact (name and phone number, e-mail or mailing address).

\#　　　　\#　　　　\#

Appendix B

Sample radio PSAs

CONTACT: (Name)   FOR IMMEDIATE RELEASE
        (Telephone)
        (Fax/e-mail)   (Date mailed)

TIME: 15 SECONDS

Service Club Golf Tournament

The fifth annual Service Club Golf Tournament will be held Tuesday, August 15, at the Woods Golf Course in Anytown. For more information on the benefit call the club at three-six-one— -20-37.

            #   #   #

TIME: 30 SECONDS

Service Club Golf Tournament

The fifth annual Service Club Golf Tournament will be held Tuesday, August 15, at the Woods Golf Course in Anytown. The

40 dollar entry fee covers greens fees, cart, and a lunch. Door prizes and goodie bags will also be provided. The money is used to fund college scholarships for local high school graduates. For more information and entry forms call the club at three-six-one—-20-37.

#   #   #

APPENDIX C

Sample forms

New Business and Promotion Form

Business name _____

Location _____

Is this a ( ) new location, ( ) expansion, ( ) promotion/award or ( ) new business?

Telephone _____ Business hours_____

Owner(s)/Manager(s)_____

_____

Services or products offered   _____

_____

_____

Other information (number of full-and part-time employees, size of facility, etc.

_____

_____

Person(s) promoted or receiving award (include new title or honor)_____

_____

_____

Background information (professional affiliations, previous employment, number of years on job, etc.) _____

_____

_____

Church News Release Form

Church name_____

Location _____

Pastor_____

Event (*Check One*) ( ) Homecoming, ( ) Singing/Concert, ( ) Revival, ( )
Bible School

( ) Other_____

Date of event_____

Speakers _____

Visiting singers_____

Name of play/film/presentation _____

_____

_____

Other information _____

_____

_____

_____

Submitted by_____**Phone** _____

Engagement Announcement

Mr. and Mrs._____ of (city and state)_____

announce the engagement of their daughter

Miss _____of (city and state) _____

to _____of (city and state) _____

son of _____of (city and state)_____

Bride-Elect's last school (circle one: attended, attending, graduated) _____

and is employed by_____

Groom-Elect's last school (circle one: attended, attending, graduated) _____

and is employed by _____

The wedding is planned for_____ at _____

Phone number to call for questions: Daytime _____ Evening _____

Parent's signature *(if either bride-elect or fiancé is underage)*

Obituary Notice

Name _____ Age_____ Address_____

Date of birth _____Place of birth _____

Date of death_____ Place of death _____

Occupation _____

Church Membership _____

Civic/Fraternal Organizations _____

Education _____Veteran _____

Father _____ Living_____

Mother _____ Living_____

Spouse_____ Living_____

Funeral Time/Date_____

Location _____ Lie in State _____

Visitation _____

Burial_____

Officiating _____

Pall Bearers_____

_____

Survivors	Relationship	Address
_____	_____	_____
_____	_____	_____
_____	_____	_____
_____	_____	_____
_____	_____	_____
_____	_____	_____
_____	_____	_____

Memorials_____

Funeral arrangements by _____

Wedding Announcement

Full name of Bride_____

Address_____

Full name of Groom _____

Address_____

Ceremony location_____hour_____

Date_____Officiating clergy_____

Names of Bride's parents_____

Address_____

Names of Groom's parents _____

Address_____

Double or single ring ceremony_____

Given in marriage by_____relation_____

Description of Bride's gown _____

_____

_____

Bride's flowers _____

_____

Maid (Matron) of Honor _____relation_____

Address_____

Bridesmaids (hometown, relation) _____

_____

_____

Best Man_____relation_____

Address_____

Ushers (hometown, relation)_____

_____

_____

Other attendants (flower girl, ring bearer, etc.)_____

_____

Director of wedding_____relation _____

Wedding music (organist, soloist, etc.)_____

_____

Time and place of reception and cake cutting_____

_____

Wedding trip destination_____

Residence after trip_____

Bride's education, occupation, background _____

_____

Groom's education, occupation, background_____

_____

Name, number of person to confirm information _____

GLOSSARY

People who don't understand the press fear it. People who do understand it fear it even more.

Jack DeVore
Cabinet press secretary
1994

There are "ads" and there are "news items" and there are even "blurbs" that newspaper editors get asked about often But the distinction between these and many other terms isn't always clear and that can cause some confusion in the world of media relations.

What follows are a few definitions that should help put readers and newspaper staff members on the same page and hopefully head off potential misunderstandings. Using these terms may also capture an editor's full attention as he wonders how an outsider managed to crack the secret code of the journalism fraternity.

Ad An abbreviation of **ad**vertising, a paid spot in the newspaper. Ads are usually divided into two categories: retail display and classified. Retail display ads are normally the larger ones that are used by businesses and are stacked from the bottom of the inside and back pages of the newspaper sections. They may also contain photos and artwork. Classified ads, also known as line ads, are usually the smaller ones dealing with help-wanted notices or items for sale. They usually appear on pages near the back of the paper or in a separate section.

If you really want to irritate an editor, just ask him about the front page "ad" that had to do with the benefit chicken dinner and had all the good stuff edited out. You can see how the confusion can already set in. First of all, an "ad" would probably not appear on the front page, and would not be edited by the paper because whatever a customer pays for in an advertisement should be used verbatim. Obviously, the chicken dinner notice referred to a news item (or blurb), which is often cleared up quite quickly when the inquiring person is asked whether it was a paid announcement.

There are some situations where the mythical free ad actually does exist, however. A newspaper may donate space to a non-profit agency or other good cause. Because of higher newsprint costs and tighter profit margins, this may not happen as often as it once did. Usually some tradeoffs or co-sponsorships are involved in free ad space deals. Newspaper promotions may also include giving away free classified advertisements in certain categories to increase the number of line ads in hopes of drawing more readers to that section.

Advertorial A paid advertisement in the form of a news article or feature story.

Art Photographs, tables, charts, graphics or drawings in a newspaper. If an editor happens to ask whether you have any "art" to go with your press release, she is not necessarily asking for a masterpiece.

Banner A headline extending across a newspaper page. Also known as a "flag."

Beat A reporter's regular assigned coverage area such as the police or education beat.

Blurb An announcement more commonly found on a book jacket than in a newspaper.

Briefs Short news items that are usually packaged together in what people in the business call a briefs package.

Broadsheet The common full format newspaper that measures about 14 inches wide by 22 inches long. (Many papers, however, are using a slightly narrower width to save newsprint.) The standard broadsheet newspaper now has six columns across the page. Some, however, still have seven and most have from eight to ten columns in the classified section.

Budget This word has a meaning besides a financial plan at newspapers. The budget or digest in the newsroom is a list of stories expected for upcoming editions. If a story is "on the budget" for that day's edition, it should be ready by deadline.

Byline The name at the beginning of an article that identifies the writer. That name may be followed by a title—such as "Staff Writer" or "Sports Editor—or by the writer's e-mail address. For a beginner or amateur writer, getting a byline is often a bigger deal than getting paid for their work (at least that's what we'd like them to believe).

Camera-ready An ad, piece of art, or block of copy in a format that needs no additional work before it can be sent back to production. Examples might be half-toned photos or color separations. (In this case "camera" doesn't refer to the hand-held equipment used by the news photographer, but to the large stationary device that is used to photograph whole newspaper pages during the plate-making process.) As more and more newspapers move toward a digital production process, the camera room is often being bypassed.

Caps An abbreviation for capital letters.

Circulation The number of newspapers distributed either through home delivery or from news racks or counter sales. It also refers to the department of the newspaper responsible for delivery.

Clarification An item intended to make clearer or expand upon a previously published story or reference. While factually correct, the original item may be seen as unfair or subject to misinterpretation.

Coding Another word for format, which is the computer language inserted into the text on the computer screen that determines how the copy will appear in the newspaper. For example a different coding might make the headlines larger and bolder than the word type in the story. (Coding is supposed to be invisible after it leaves the computer screen but sometimes you can catch some of it in print due to a processing error. If you see some letters or numbers that look out of place amid the words of a story, somebody's coding may be showing.)

Composing The department that actually puts together the pages from the designs provided by the editors and advertising department. Many composing departments do this by cutting and pasting the copy onto sheets, but many more are now doing the cutting and pasting electronically on computer screens.

Copy Any words submitted or produced for publication. Example: "Johnson, where's your copy on the poodle who drove his sick owner to the hospital?" or "They finally turned in the copy on the assistant school janitor of the year award."

Correction An item intended to correct a factual error in a previously published story.

Credit line Usually placed below or beside a photograph, illustration or graphic to identify the person who took the photo or created the art.

Crop The process by which unwanted areas are eliminated from photos. This can be done electronically to a digital image on the computer or physically with a knife, razor blade or other cutting tool on a halftone. This is how editors make the subject of the photo more prominent by getting rid of wasted space beside, below or above the subject.

Cutline A word most newspaper people use instead of photo caption. It means the information or copy that goes with the photograph to identify subjects and explain what the image is about.

Dateline Words used at the beginning of a news story or press release to show where the story originated, but not necessarily where it was written. For example, a reporter who is doing a telephone interview from

Hudson, N.Y. about a news event going on in the state capital might use an ALBANY, N.Y. dateline. (Strangely enough, a dateline often doesn't include the date.)

Deadline The latest time by which news stories must be completed, advertisements scheduled and prepared, pages made up, and press runs made.

Digital A format that can be read, altered, transferred and stored by computer. It is the form that many stories, ads and photographs are in before being put on the printed newspaper page. An article in a computer database is in digital form, which allows it to be easily edited and its style changed to suit the needs of a variety of newspaper formats.

Down-style The way we would like to see all press releases and other submissions come in. Only the first letter of the first word in the sentence and proper nouns are capitalized and all other letters are in lower case. It is the opposite of "up-style" or "all-caps."

Dummy (It's nothing personal.) The drawn guide that the printer or composing person follows to produce the page designed by the editor. It also means to draw such a guide. For example, an editor might say, "I have to dummy the page one dummy for today's paper." This is one area where low-tech tools are still commonly used—a pencil and sheet of paper. But with more and more newspapers going to electronic pagination, a lot of dummying is being done on the computer screen.

Ear An expression used to describe the areas at the top corners of the front page where information or art is sometimes inserted. So if an editor says she is going to take your copy and "stick it in the ear," be pleased rather than offended because it is getting a prime position.

Edition All copies of a newspaper printed at one time without typographic changes. This term should not be confused with "issue," which means all of the newspapers printed in one day, consisting of one or more editions. So while two customers of the *Daily Spider* may have gotten the same issue, the customer who received the later edition of the paper was the only one to get the results of the late World Series game.

Editor The hapless man or woman who is responsible for all or part of the news operation. Depending on the size of the newspapers, the editor can be a specialist or generalist. Most titles are self-explanatory—Sports Editor, Lifestyles Editor, Religion Editor. Duties of some editors vary from paper to paper with community and local news usually coming under the jurisdiction of a News Editor or City Editor.

The Pensacola News-Journal defines an editor as the person whose job it is to exercise good judgment in determining what is of most interest to the most readers through the newspaper's circulation area. Susan Deans, editor of *The Sun News* of Myrtle Beach, S.C., was able to describe what she does every day in one word.

"Mom."

She explains: "Well, having been a mom, there are a lot of similarities. You are constantly trying to nurture—in this case an organization that puts out a new product every day. You don't have much time to think about it. You are never quite sure you are doing the right thing, and it takes a long time and a lot of perspective to see whether you have succeeded."

Editorial A stuffy way of referring to the news department, and also the term used for the commentary pieces that appear, of all places, on the Editorial Page. Editorials are supposed to reflect the corporate opinion of the paper's editorial board, reflecting the paper's position on a variety of issues. Editorials are not to be confused, but often are, with letters to the editor that are opinion statements submitted by readers. "Editorial matter" also refers to everything in the newspaper except for the advertising.

Evergreen A description of feature material that isn't time-sensitive. For example, a story about a historical event that would have the same impact whether it is published tomorrow or next month. Community newspaper editors, especially those at small papers who don't have wire service copy to rely on, like to have a few of these pieces around as insurance. The stories come in handy when an editor is confronted with some space to fill on deadline and no fresh news copy to fill it.

Feature A newspaper article that may not be considered breaking or hard news. An example would be a story on a local resident's prized vegetable garden.

Filing What editors and reporters often call turning in a story. When a reporter finishes the story and turns it over to the editor the story is filed.

Hard copy Copy printed out on paper. It is the tangible form as opposed to digital words on the computer screen. If something has been lost in the computer system or dumped from the computer memory, an editor will hope there is a hard copy available to be typeset or scanned back into the system.

Headshot Also called a "mug shot," a headshot is a photo of a person that focuses on the face, head and top of the shoulders.

Headline Large type used at the beginning of a story that gives the reader a quick indication of what the story is about. (Also called "a head" for short). The size of a headline is often an indication of the story's importance. Summarizing an entire news story in just a few words is one of the biggest challenges for editors.

House ad An advertisement that is generated by the newspaper to fill an unsold spot or to advertise something the paper wants to promote.

Index The table of contents for a newspaper. It usually appears on the front page.

Insert As a noun, a single sheet or section included in the regular edition of a newspaper, usually an advertising flier or supplement. As a verb, the act of putting this material into the newspaper.

Issue All copies of newspapers printed in one day.

Jump A term used to describe the part of a story that is continued from one page to another. For example, a story on a proposed landfill could start on the front page and "jump" to page seven. Jumps are also commonly called "runovers," or as the late editor Janelou Buck used to call them "slopovers." The term "jump" is also used to describe the act of continuing a story to another page. Example: "I'm going to jump this murder story from page one to page three."

Layout Another term for the page design and can also refer to the composing room. Example: "We've already got the layout done, and it's back in layout so I don't think we can change anything now."

Lead (pronounced "lede") The first paragraph of an article that is designed to draw the reader into the story.

Makeup The general style in which elements are arranged on the newspaper page.

Masthead The part of a newspaper stating the names of the publisher, owner, and editors, the location of the business, advertising and editorial offices, mailing address and other information. Many newspapers position this information on page 2.

Morgue The place where old newspapers are traditionally stored. Many papers now maintain back issues in microfilm libraries or electronic archives that can be accessed online.

Mug shot Also called a "head shot," this is a photo of a person that focuses on the face, head and top of the shoulders. For example, an editor may ask, "Do you have a mug of the guest speaker to send with your press release?"

Nameplate The part of the newspaper that identifies it by name or logo and is located near the top of the front page.

Op-ed Used to refer to the page opposite the editorial page. The op-ed page is usually used for additional commentary. Smaller papers that only have one page of commentary may still refer out of habit to pieces as op-ed even if that copy appears on the editorial page rather than the facing page.

Pagination Refers to electronic composition of pages. The words, photos, headlines and graphics are put together on the computer screen and are sent out to the printer or printing press plate maker as one piece.

Pica A common unit of measurement used by newspapers, although inches are also widely used. There are six picas to the inch.

Proof As a noun, an early printout of copy or a page used for checking for errors. As a verb, the act of checking the printed copy for errors.

Pub date A shorthand way of saying publication date.

Publisher The person who heads the entire operation. At smaller papers, he or she can be both the publisher and editor.

ROP A term that stands for run-of-paper and refers to news and advertising that can appear on any page or section in the paper.

Scan The way many traditional photographs or photo negatives are made into digital images and put into the computer. It is also a way that copy can be put into digital form without having a person type it into a database.

Sidebar A closely related story that goes along with a more prominent piece. For example, if you were to submit a very long and detailed story about an auto show, an editor might break it into two stories—the main one about the show and a sidebar about the organizer or some other specific aspect of the event. This related piece is often set to the side of the main story or boxed with lines.

Slug. The name a story or news release is given so that it can be noted on the dummy sheet and be identified and retrieved when it is put into the computer system. For example, the story about the poodle driver may simply be slugged "poodle." On common story slugs such as "city" and "murder," a number may also be added to differentiate it so that an editor knows that "city5.23" is the city story that was written for the May 23 issue.

Stand-alone This refers to a photo that is published without an accompanying story. This is also known as a "self-contained" photo or "wild art."

Stringer A person contracted by a newspaper to cover specific events or stories. This is a person who is not a part of the regular news staff but augments the staff by doing freelance work. Stringers, who can also be known as correspondents, are often paid by the job rather than by the hour.

Style A standard of literary or typographic usage for a publication. For example, a newspaper in one town always capitalizes the word "Race" when referring to the city's big annual auto racing event.

Normally the word when used alone is lower case, but it is the *style* of that newspaper to capitalize it.

Subhead A headline that goes below the main headline in smaller type and provides more information about the story that follows it. Subheads are also used to break up long stories by dividing each of them into sections.

Syndicate A company that represents writers, artists or other features and sells their services to publications. Most cartoon strips and editorial and advice columnists, and features such as horoscopes and crossword puzzles that appear in newspapers are supplied by syndicates rather than by in-house staff members. For example, if you called up the *Daily Crawdad* and asked to speak to columnist Andy Rooney you would be told that his column is syndicated and that he doesn't work at every paper in which his writing appears.

As a verb, syndicate can mean to sell an article through such an arrangement.

Tabloid A newspaper format in which the pages are half the size of the standard broadsheet. Called a "tab" for short, the newspapers in this format have been traditionally known for a more flashy approach to news reporting. Some well-known tabs in the United States are *The New York Daily News* and *The National Enquirer*. Tabloids may also appear in broadsheet newspapers as special sections. For example, many papers insert special tabloid sections on entertainment or business on a weekly basis.

Tear sheet A page separated—or torn—from a newspaper as proof of publication.

Teaser A headline or copy used on the front of a section intended to attract the reader to the full story inside.

Thumbnail An expression used to describe a half-column (1 by 11/2-inch) photo, usually a mug shot.

Typesetter This word also has a dual meaning. It can mean both the machine that turns digital copy into hard copy on film or paper, or it can mean the person whose job it is to type or otherwise transfer hard copy into the computer database.

Typo Just a fancy way of saying we goofed in our typesetting. It's just one of the many potential mistakes that can be made at a newspaper.

Wire services Companies that supply information and images to newspapers by way of satellite transmissions or telephone lines. Most notable among these is the Associated Press, which provides most newspapers with much of their world, national and state news stories.

Zoned editions Newspapers delivered to different areas and that contain news and advertising specifically targeted at readers in those areas.

This was a quick lesson in newspaper jargon and is certainly not all-inclusive. Some newspapers make their own terms and names for processes and tools as they need them. For the most part, however, the terms are the industry standard for all papers.

References

Text references

AJR American Journalism Review, College of Journalism of the University of Maryland at College Park, Adelphi, Md., October, 1997.

Arnold, Ed, Modern Newspaper Design, New York: McGraw-Hill Book Co., 1968.

Associated Press Style Manual, The Associated Press, New York, NY. 1998.

Bradlee, Ben, A Good Life: Newspapering And Other Adventures, Simon & Schuster, New York, 1995, p. 430.

Chicago Manual of Style, 14th Edition, The University of Chicago Press, Chicago, 1993, p. 295.

Davidson, J., Becoming Your Own Press Agent. The Rangefinder, 1985, p. 34.

Carnegie, Dale, How To Win Friends & Influence People, Simon And Schuster, New York, 1981, p.102.

Davidson, Jim, You Can Be The Best, Continuing Educational Services, Inc., Conway, Ark., 1991, p. 42.

Gottfried, John, Giving The Media Food For Thought, Nation's Business, September 1996, p.6.

Internet Routine For Newsroom, *Editor & Publisher*, March 8, 1997, p. 49.

Newspaper Association of America, *1999 Facts About Newspapers Newsroom Lore*, The Freedom Forum, 1999.

Palmer, Cruise, Today's Editor: marketer, cheerleader, parent, *The American Editor*, June 1997.

Parachin, Victor M., From 'Merchant of Death' to architect of peace—the story of Alfred Nobel, *The Rotarian*, November 1997, p. 18.

Presstime, May 1997.

Presstime, March 2000.

Rooney, Andrew A., *Word for Word*, New York: G.P. Putnam's Sons, 1986.

Shepard, Alicia C., Blowing up the Wall, *American Journalism Review*, December 1997, p. 20.

Smith, Jeanette, *The Publicity Kit*, John Wiley and Sons, Inc., 1991, Sova, Dawn B., *How to write articles for newspapers and magazines*, Macmillan Reference USA, New York, N.Y., 1998.

Stein, M.L., Still Jabbing at the Press, *Editor & Publisher*, Oct. 25, 1997, p. 29.

Strunk, William, Jr., and White, E.B., *The Elements of Style,* Simon 7 Schuster Company, Needham Heights, Massachusetts, 1979.

Strupp, Joe, Playing the numbers game, *Editor & Publisher*, March 6, 2000, p. 20.

Survey: Americans Don't Trust Media, *The* (Southern Newspaper Association) *Bulletin*, March 15, 1997, p. 8.

Zagorin, Adam, Taking Stock Scams Off-line, *Time* magazine, March 13, 2000, p. 60.

Internet references

Arizona Daily Courier, AZ http://www.prescottaz.com/pdc/courier.htm
Arkansas Democrat Gazette, AR http://www.ardemgaz.com
Bakersfield Californian, Bakersfield, CA http://www.kern.com/tbc/

Birmingham Post-Herald, Birmingham, AL http://www.postherald.com

Charlottesville Albermerle Observer, Charlottesville, VA http://www.igfmedia.com/observer/

Columbus Ledger-Enquirer, Columbia, GE http://www.l-e-o.com

Daily Press, Victorville, CA http://www.vvdailypress.com

Daily Republic, Fairfield, CA http://www.dailyrepublic.com

Davis Enterprise, Davis CA http://www.

Honolulu Star-Bulletin, Honolulu, HA http://www.starbulletin.com

LaGrange Daily News, LaGrange, GE http://www.lagrangenews.com

Los Angeles Times, Los Angeles CA http://www.latimes.com

Mobile Register, Mobile AL http://www.mobileregister.com

Newark Post, Newark, DE http://www.ncbl.com/post/

News & Record, Greensboro, NC http://www.greensboro.com

Orlando Sentinel, Orlando, FL http://www.orlandosentinel.com

Sacramento Bee, Sacramento, CA http://www.sacbee.com

Savannah Morning News, Savannah, GE http://www.savannahnow.com

Slipup.com, http://www.Slipup.com

Sun Sentinel, Ft. Lauderdale, FL http://www.sun-sentinel.com

Tampa Tribune, Tampa, FL http://www.tampatrib.com